SPEAKING
OF
SURVIVAL

DANIEL B. FREEMAN

OXFORD UNIVERSITY PRESS

Oxford University Press

200 Madison Avenue
New York, N.Y. 10016 USA

Walton Street
Oxford OX2 6DP England

OXFORD is a trademark of Oxford University Press.

Library of Congress Cataloging in Publication Data

Freeman, Daniel B., 1920—
    Speaking of survival.

    1. English language—Text-books for foreigners.
I. Title.
PE1128.F68   428.3′4   81-18692
ISBN 0-19-503110-5 (pbk.)   AACR2

Illustrations by Jack Fetchko for flex, Inc.

Printing (last digit): 10 9

Printed in Hong Kong

Acknowledgments

Grateful acknowledgments are due to the many people who have encouraged me in the writing of this book. In particular I am indebted to E. C. Parnwell (*Oxford Picture Dictionary of American English*), Dr. J. C. Richards (*Conversation in Action*), and Jill Schimpff (*Open Sesame Picture Dictionary*) for inspiring some of the format of this book. I also wish to thank my students at the American Language Center at the College of Mount Saint Vincent for acting as a sounding board during the many trial versions of the book.

Special thanks are due to Dr. Irwin Feigenbaum (University of Texas at Arlington) and Dr. Robert Fox (American University) for their many helpful comments and suggestions. Thanks also go to Professor Mary Ann Hood (American University), Dr. Carol Cargill-Powers (University of Florida), and Allene Grognet (Center for Applied Linguistics) for their sound advice.

I am especially grateful to Dr. Marilyn Rosenthal for her inestimable assistance in the editing of this manuscript. Thanks also to Debra Sistino, Vicky Bijur, Lenore Schaefer, and Connie Attanasio for their many efforts on behalf of the manuscript.

Lulu Freeman, whose bark was often worse than her bite, contributed more than she will ever know.

I am very grateful to my wife, Sylvia, for her patience and understanding during the many hours it took to write this book.

Riverdale, N.Y.   D.B.F.
January 1982

Contents

To the Teacher

Speaking of Survival is a course designed for adult learners of English as a Second Language (ESL) at the high beginner/low intermediate level. It is particularly addressed to newcomers to the United States and presents the basic survival contexts all newcomers must cope with.

S.O.S. is based on the premise that although the language level of the student may be in the developmental stages, his* intellectual capacity is that of an adult. **S.O.S.**, therefore, makes very conscious attempts to treat the learner with dignity and to appeal to his cognitive competence, curiosity, and need for practical, helpful information in the real situations he will face.

That is, **S.O.S.** presents the linguistic forms and functions of English as well as the actual information and advice adults need in order to function comfortably.

S.O.S. may be used as the basic text in a non-intensive three- to six-hour a week program or as part of a curriculum in an intensive twenty-hour ESL program.

The Finger Index on the front cover provides a handy guide for locating the beginning of each unit. Simply align the arrow of any of the tabs with the corresponding mark on the sides of the pages (between the two covers of the book) to open the book to the unit of your choice. The book is not designed to be used developmentally, though you may use it that way. Structures are presented spirally, so each unit may be used as needed.

THE ORGANIZATION OF EACH UNIT

Each unit is self-contained and presents the four language skills of listening, speaking, reading, and writing.

The focus of each unit is a particular survival situation. The language functions, grammar, vocabulary, and cultural information are presented in the context of each situation.

The following chart illustrates the development of the unit.

*Apologies are made for the generalized use of the masculine pronoun. It is meant to be used for simplicity's sake, rather than to indicate a philosophical viewpoint. I feel that the *s/he*, *her/him*, *his/her* forms, while they may be philosophically appealing, are confusing.

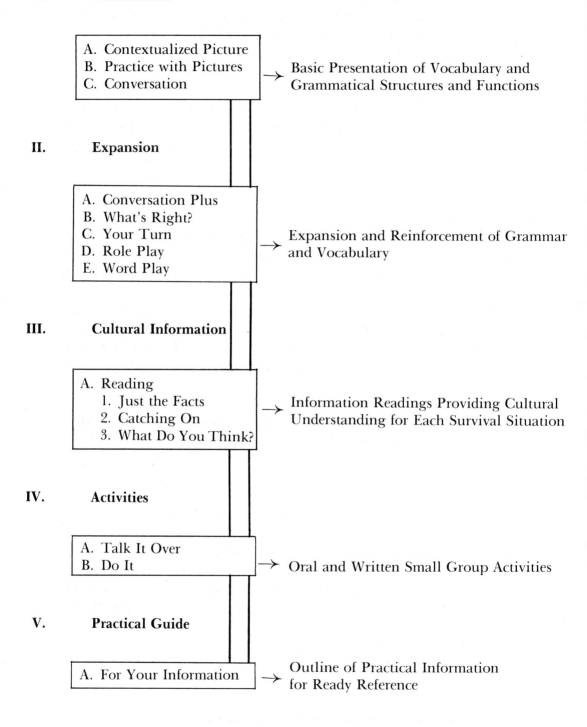

I.   Presentation

> A. Contextualized Picture
> B. Practice with Pictures   → Basic Presentation of Vocabulary and
> C. Conversation   Grammatical Structures and Functions

II.   Expansion

> A. Conversation Plus
> B. What's Right?
> C. Your Turn   → Expansion and Reinforcement of Grammar
> D. Role Play   and Vocabulary
> E. Word Play

III.   Cultural Information

> A. Reading
>   1. Just the Facts   → Information Readings Providing Cultural
>   2. Catching On   Understanding for Each Survival Situation
>   3. What Do You Think?

IV.   Activities

> A. Talk It Over
> B. Do It   → Oral and Written Small Group Activities

V.   Practical Guide

> A. For Your Information   → Outline of Practical Information
>   for Ready Reference

The **Presentation** section of every unit consists of a full-color contextualized illustration depicting the basic vocabulary the student will encounter. Further vocabulary, both productive and receptive, is presented in individualized pictures in Practice with Pictures. Two pages of conversation typical of the functional language used in each situation follow.

The **Expansion** section provides oral and written exercises which exploit and reinforce the vocabulary and structures just introduced in the **Presentation** section. Exercises here consist of substitution practice, matching sentences for appropriateness, question and answer practice, role play, and word play. These exercises lead the student, in a systematic progression, toward free conversation.

The **Cultural Information** section generally consists of two Readings, each providing cultural information, including sound emergency advice. The Readings are followed by true/false questions, information questions, and opinion questions, which also provide opportunities for the students to compare their own cultures.

The **Activities** section provides small group or individualized activities. Talk It Over gives the students an opportunity to discuss their values and to do oral mini-questionnaires. Do It provides written practice in using coping skills they will need, such as looking up emergency numbers, using the *Yellow Pages*, and figuring dollar saving on unit pricing in the super-market.

The **Practical Guide** section at the end of each unit is a one-page outline of very helpful information. The student can rely on this as a ready reference when needed.

SUGGESTIONS FOR PRESENTING EACH UNIT

Although all good classroom teachers have developed their own techniques for individualizing ESL texts to suit their students' particular needs, it might be useful to list the basic purpose and some suggestions for presentation for each of the parts of the unit in working through the book.

A. The Contextualized Picture:

Purpose: to set the general framework for each particular topic. To provide the basic vocabulary that the student will encounter in each survival situation.

Presentation: The vocabulary may be presented through choral and individual repetition, as well as through cued response, in which the teacher says the numbers and the students say the words. For more advanced students, the teacher might use the picture to stimulate discussion or to ask questions about a particular scene. For example, in Unit 1, there is a picture of a doctor using a tongue depressor and a flashlight on a patient. A nurse behind him is reading a thermometer. The teacher might ask, "What is the doctor doing?", "What is the nurse doing?", "What is the patient doing?"

B. Practice with Pictures:

Purpose: to extend the vocabulary to those words that might not be found in the contextualized picture.

Presentation: Since this is an extension of what has already been done in the contextualized picture, the teacher may use the same presentation ideas. It should be noted that many of the words might be useful to the students simply to allay fears, if they should come across them in the particular situation. For example, it may not be necessary for students to be able to say "Novocaine," but they should be familiar with the item as well as the word, so that they won't be troubled when presented by it in the situation. The teacher can decide which of the vocabulary might be more useful for receptive vs. productive competence.

C. Conversation:

Purpose: to practice conversational exchanges that might be typically used in each survival situation. Each unit generally has two conversations, although at times there is one long conversation instead. Several structures are presented simultaneously, and the conversations are more communicatively and functionally based than structurally based.

Presentation: The teacher should present the Conversation first and ask if there are any questions. Then the students may repeat, chorally, individually, or in small groups. Another variation is to have student-to-student practice in which each group of two students practices the conversation together. It is possible with large classes to have all the students simultaneously working in pairs.

D. Conversation Plus:

Purpose: to expand and reinforce the material presented in the Conversation. This leads the student from the more tightly controlled repetition in the conversation to the first step in the lessening of controls, in which the student is substituting new vocabulary into previously presented sentences. Conversation Plus is a substitution drill taking sentences already presented in the Conversation and introducing new vocabulary into these previously learned sentences.

Presentation: The teacher should present the first sentence and the first example of the vocabulary to be substituted. For example,

> T: "I want to go to Kraft Street." (the bus stop)
>
> Ss: "I want to go to the bus stop."
>
> T: (the airport)
>
> Ss: "I want to go to the airport."

E. What's Right?:

Purpose: to teach linguistic appropriateness in a two-person dialog exchange. Sometimes the student selects the appropriate response when given the question; sometimes he selects the appropriate question when given the response. The questions and responses here all come from the dialog.

Presentation: The teacher may present the question and have the students select the appropriate response or may present the response and have the students select the appropriate question. This exercise may also be done student-to-student.

F. Your Turn:

Purpose: Although this is based on the Conversation, the student has an opportunity to respond freely to either the question or the answer which was originally in the Conversation. Here the students can either give a previously remembered model from the Conversation or provide their own appropriate answer, depending on the needs and nature of the class.

Presentation: The teacher might ask the question and the student would respond either with a sentence from the dialog or with his own free answer. This can also be done student-to-student.

G. Role Play:

Purpose: for the student to be able to respond freely in a simulated survival situation. The students role-play each part of a typical conversation. The roles that they are playing are similar to those already presented in the Conversation, but here there are no models to choose from. There are only cues which set the scene.

Presentation: The teacher reads the cues given in the exercise. Two students take the roles. Corrections can be made at the end of each two-student role play. The teacher might divide the class into groups of two students role-playing simultaneously, while going around, listening to, and correcting each pair.

H. Word Play:

Purpose: to give students reinforcement and practice with the words previously presented in the Contextualized Picture and/or the Practice with Pictures. There are two types of word play exercises: the first is categories, where the students select the one word that does not match the other three in the group; for example, stomach-eye-hand-pills. In another type of word play exercise, the students use words from the vocabulary list in four sentences. Some words are appropriate to one sentence-type, some are appropriate to another sentence-type. For example:

Sentences

"My _____ hurts."
"Take the _____ three times a day."

Word List

Stomach
Pills
Eye
Capsules

I. Reading:

Purpose: to give practical information relevant to the survival topic. The Reading introduces new vocabulary along with longer sentence structure more characteristic of that used in the written language.

Presentation: The teacher reads the selection once. The books are open, so students can have practice associating the spoken language with the written language. Another variation is for students to take turns reading without the teacher model. The teacher might also want to use simply silent reading. After each reading, there are factual or opinion questions.

J. Just the Facts:
Purpose: to provide a comprehension check on the reading. This exercise is the most structured of the question-and-answer exercises after the Reading. It is a true-false exercise. The teacher, however, may lead the class into a discussion by simply using the word "why."

Presentation: The teacher reads and the students say true-false, or one student reads and the other students say true-false.

K. Catching On:
Purpose: to provide a comprehension check on the story. Catching On presents information questions using *who, what, where, why*, or *when*. These types of questions allow the student to use more vocabulary and grammar in his response than true-false questions. The linguistic sophistication of the response depends on the individual student. However, even beginning students may find the actual answer in the reading selection.

Presentation: The teacher asks the questions and the students answer, or the students read the questions and other students answer them.

L. What Do You Think?:
Purpose: to stimulate discussion and to have the students speak freely regarding what they are feeling. The teacher can expand the discussion generated by the questions if he emphasizes the "why" or "why not" part.

Presentation: The teacher asks the students questions or the students ask each other questions. The students may also ask the teacher questions. This is a wonderful opportunity for cultural comparisons and for the students to express themselves creatively.

M. Talk It Over:
Purpose: This is a communicative activity which allows the students to use the language for information purposes. Here they have the opportunity to investigate or discuss a problem pertaining to each survival topic. In order to do this, they must use the language to relate to each other as well as to native speakers outside the classroom. Each activity in the Talk It Over section of

a unit differs depending on the topic at hand. All, however, include small group activities or pair work.

Presentation: This activity is almost totally student-centered. The teacher may help set up the groups and correct the students' English when needed. Corrections should be limited in order not to interfere with the spontaneity of the students.

N. Do It:

Purpose: to reinforce writing and research skills as individual written work or homework. Some of the Do It activities provide practice in alphabetizing and information retrieval. They are student-centered. The teacher can correct students' work and make suggestions for further practice. The Do It exercises give students practical experience with looking up items and other coping skills which they might have to perform in survival situations.

O. For Your Information:

Purpose: to present capsulized practical information in outline form, which would be comprehensive, for each survival situation. This can be used as an information guide, sometimes providing a ready reference for students to actually carry with them. Much of this information is consumer-oriented. For Your Information can also be used as an oral activity, providing the teacher with a tool for expanding class discussion.

Presentation: The teacher might do a comprehension check of the For Your Information section by asking "yes-no" and "information questions." The teacher could also lead a discussion which would be stimulated by the list of information in the For Your Information section.

As you work through each Unit, many more ideas for presentation will develop. We invite you to share them.

THE DOCTOR

The Doctor

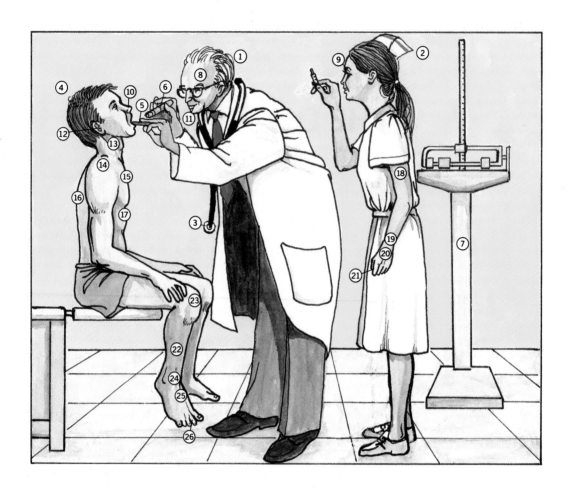

1. doctor
2. nurse
3. stethoscope
4. patient
5. tongue depressor
6. flashlight
7. scale
8. head
9. eye
10. nose
11. mouth
12. ear
13. neck
14. shoulder
15. chest
16. back
17. stomach
18. arm
19. wrist
20. hand
21. finger
22. leg
23. knee
24. ankle
25. foot
26. toe

PRACTICE WITH PICTURES

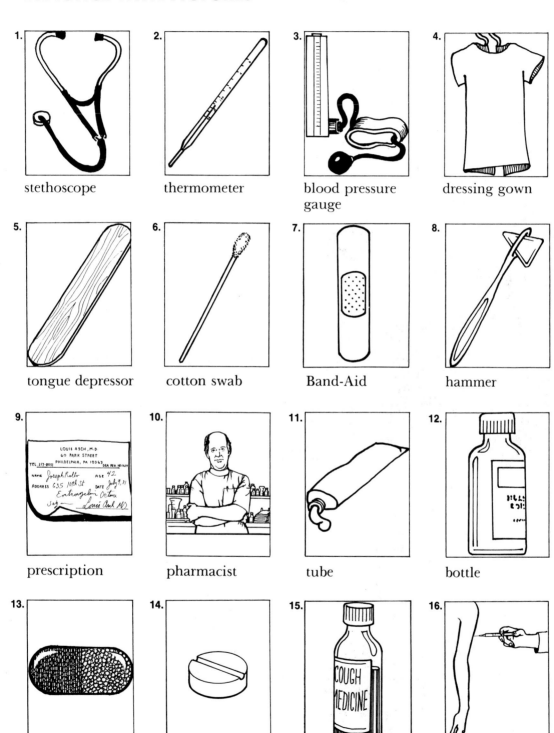

1. stethoscope

2. thermometer

3. blood pressure gauge

4. dressing gown

5. tongue depressor

6. cotton swab

7. Band-Aid

8. hammer

9. prescription

10. pharmacist

11. tube

12. bottle

13. capsule

14. pill/tablet

15. cough medicine

16. injection

CONVERSATION 1: Going for an Examination

1.

A. How do you feel, Mr. Salazar?
B. I feel fine. I need a check-up.

2.

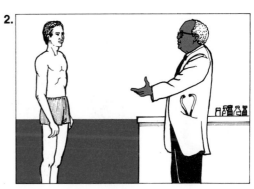

A. Take off your clothes, but keep
   your shorts on.
B. Okay.

3.

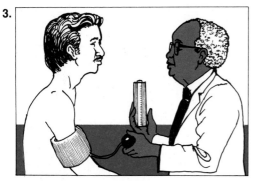

B. What's that?
A. It measures your blood pressure.

4.

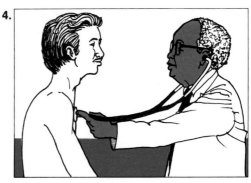

A. Your heart is okay.
B. Great.

5.

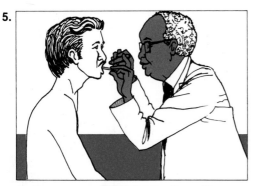

A. Let me see your throat. Say, Ah.
B. Ah.

6.

A. You're very healthy.
B. Thanks, Doctor.

CONVERSATION 2: Feeling Sick

1.

A. My stomach hurts.
B. When did it start?
A. This morning.

2.

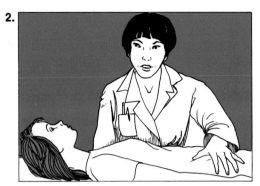

B. Does it hurt when I touch your
    stomach?
A. A little.

3.

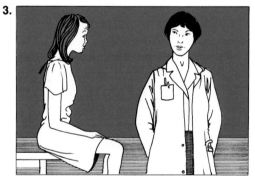

B. You might have appendicitis.
A. Is that dangerous?

4.

B. Maybe, I'll take some tests.
A. Do I have to go to the hospital?
B. No.

5.

B. Your tests are negative, so you're
    okay.
A. But I still have pain in my
    stomach.

6.

B. I'll give you a prescription for some
    pills. Take the pills three times a day.
A. Thanks, Doctor.

CONVERSATION PLUS

Use the words in parentheses in each sentence below to make new sentences.

1. I feel **fine**. (*okay, good, great, sick, terrible, awful*)
2. Your **heart** is okay. (*chest, stomach, back, shoulder*)
3. **You're** very healthy. (*We're, They're*)
4. **She's** very healthy. (*He's, Joe's, Fran's*)
5. My **stomach** hurts. (*head, leg, back, arm*)
6. Take the pills **three times a day**. (*twice a day, every 6 hours, after every meal*)
7. Is that **dangerous**? (*safe, good, bad*)
8. **I'll** take some tests. (*We'll, He'll, She'll, You'll, They'll*)

WHAT'S RIGHT?

Make the *appropriate* choice. Choose a, b, or c for each number below.

1. How do you feel?
   - ☐ a. A little.
   - ☐ b. I feel fine.
   - ☐ c. Ah.

2. Your heart is okay.
   - ☐ a. Great.
   - ☐ b. I have a pain in my stomach.
   - ☐ c. What can I do?

3. ☐ a. Let me see your throat.   Thanks, Doctor.
   ☐ b. Take off your clothes.
   ☐ c. You're very healthy.

4. ☐ a. Your heart is okay.   Ah!
   ☐ b. Say, Ah!
   ☐ c. Does it hurt when I touch
       your stomach?

5. ☐ a. When did it start?   This morning.
   ☐ b. What's that?
   ☐ c. Is that dangerous?

6. Does it hurt when I touch your   ☐ a. Three times a day.
   stomach?   ☐ b. A little.
                                         ☐ c. Thanks, Doctor.

7. Do I have to go to the hospital?   ☐ a. Great.
                                         ☐ b. Okay.
                                         ☐ c. No.

YOUR TURN

Fill in each blank with an appropriate question or answer.

1. A. How do you feel?
   B. _____

2. A. Your heart is okay.
   B. _____

3. A. You're very healthy.
   B. _____

4. A. _____
   B. This morning.

5. A. Does it hurt when I touch your stomach?
   B. _____

6. A. _____
   B. Is that dangerous?

7. A. _____
   B. Thanks, Doctor.

ROLE PLAY

1. You have a pain in your stomach and you go to the doctor. You tell the doctor the problem and the doctor helps you.

   You: _____

   Doctor: _____

   You: _____

   Doctor: _____

   You: _____

   Doctor: _____

2. You go to the doctor for a check-up. The doctor asks you how you feel and you tell him.

   Doctor: _____

   You: _____

   Doctor: _____

   You: _____

   Doctor: _____

   You: _____

WORD PLAY

Complete the sentences below with the *appropriate* word from the Word List. You can use some words in more than one sentence.

Sentences

a. My _____ hurts.

b. Take these _____ three times a day.

c. What's that? It's a _____.

d. She'll examine your _____.

Word List

1. stomach
2. pills
3. eye
4. hand
5. stethoscope
6. Band-Aid
7. capsules
8. tongue depressor
9. ear
10. shoulder
11. ankle
12. knee
13. thermometer
14. cotton swab

READING 1: A Check-up

You should go to a doctor for a check-up once a year. This will prevent* serious* illness*. The doctor will examine you. He'll check your eyes, your ears, and your throat. He'll listen to your heart and lungs. He'll take your blood pressure. Tell him how you feel. The doctor will tell you if there is anything wrong. Most of the time everything will be fine. Health insurance covers some medical expenses. Get a health insurance form from your employer and bring it to the doctor.

*prevent — stop before it happens
*serious — very bad
*illness — sickness

Just the Facts

Tell whether the following statements are true or false.

1. You should go to the doctor only when you are sick.

2. A check-up can prevent serious illness.

3. You shouldn't tell the doctor anything.

4. The doctor will examine you to find out what is wrong.

5. Most of the time everything will be fine.

READING 2: If You Are Sick

When you don't feel well, call a doctor. Tell him what is wrong. Tell him how you feel. The doctor will diagnose* the problem. He will give you a prescription for medicine. Take the prescription to the drugstore. If you have any questions, ask the doctor.

If you don't feel better in a day or two, call the doctor again. If you feel very sick and can't find a doctor, go to the nearest hospital emergency room.

*diagnose — find out what is wrong

Catching On

Answer the following questions.

1. What should you do when you don't feel well?
2. What should you tell the doctor?
3. What will the doctor do?
4. Where do you get a prescription?
5. Where do you take a prescription?
6. If you have any questions, who do you ask?
7. What do you do if you can't find a doctor?

What Do You Think?

Answer the following questions.

1. Do you think a check-up is a good idea? Tell why or why not.
2. When do you call the doctor?
3. Who pays medical expenses in your country?
4. Should medical treatment be free? Tell why or why not.
5. Do you prefer a male or female doctor? Tell why.
6. Do you prefer a young or old doctor? Tell why.

TALK IT OVER

Ask three people the questions below. Share this information with the class.

Questions	1	2	3
1. What do you do when you're sick?			
2. Do you go to the doctor for check-ups?			
3. Do you take pills often?			
4. How often are you sick?			
5. Do you do what the doctor tells you?			
6. Do you have medical insurance?			
7. Should medical care be free?			

DO IT

Below is a list of directions for using medicine you can buy in a drugstore. Read the labels on the products below. Put the name of the *appropriate* product next to each direction.

Hackley Cough Medicine

Take one tea-spoon after every meal. Do not take more than four teaspoons a day.

Young's Aspirin

For headaches take two tablets every four hours. Do not take more than 12 tablets a day.

Robert's Foot Powder

Shake powder into shoes every morning. Do not get powder in your eyes.

Ames Skin Cream

Apply to skin to relieve itching. Do not apply to sunburned skin.

Muscle Ease
Rub on sore muscles for relief of pain. Do not apply to cuts.

Seltzer Plus
For stomach pain dissolve one tablet in a glass of water. Do not give to children.

Product	Directions
_____	1. Do not give to children.
_____	2. Shake powder into shoes every morning.
_____	3. Do not take more than four teaspoons a day
_____	4. Do not apply to cuts.
_____	5. Take two tablets every four hours.
_____	6. Rub on sore muscles for relief of pain.
_____	7. Do not apply to sunburned skin.
_____	8. Do not take more than 12 tablets a day.
_____	9. Apply to skin to relieve itching.
_____	10. Dissolve one tablet in a glass of water.
_____	11. Do not get powder in your eyes.
_____	12. Take one teaspoon after every meal.

FOR YOUR INFORMATION

A. To find a doctor:

1. Ask a neighbor.
2. Look in the *Yellow Pages* of the telephone book.
3. Call the State Medical Society. You can find this number in the *White Pages* of the telephone book.

B. If you can't find a doctor:

Go to the nearest hospital.

C. There are many kinds of doctors. Some doctors are specialists. This means they are experts in one branch of medicine. The list below shows some of the special kinds of doctors. There are more. Your doctor can tell you which specialist to see for any problem.

Specialist	Specialty
1. Pediatrician	Babies and Children
2. Internist	Nonsurgical Diseases
3. Obstetrician	Pregnancies and Childbirth
4. Orthopedist	Bones
5. Psychiatrist	Nervous Problems
6. Radiologist	Use of X-rays
7. Ophthalmologist	Diseases of the Eye

D. Getting a second opinion:

If you are not sure that your doctor is right, see another doctor. It is important to do this if you are seriously ill. Your medical insurance will pay for this. Your doctor should understand the need for a second opinion and respect it.

THE HOSPITAL
EMERGENCY ROOM

The Hospital Emergency Room

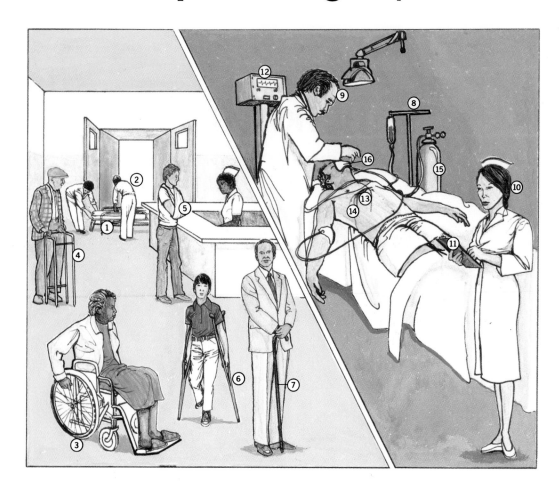

1. stretcher
2. paramedic
3. wheelchair
4. walker
5. sling
6. crutch
7. cane
8. I.V./intravenous
9. surgeon
10. nurse
11. chart
12. EKG/electrocardiograph
13. wound
14. blood
15. oxygen
16. mask

PRACTICE WITH PICTURES

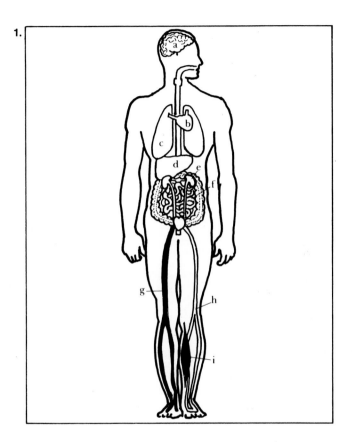

a. brain

b. heart

c. lung

d. liver

e. kidney

f. intestines

g. vein

h. artery

i. muscle

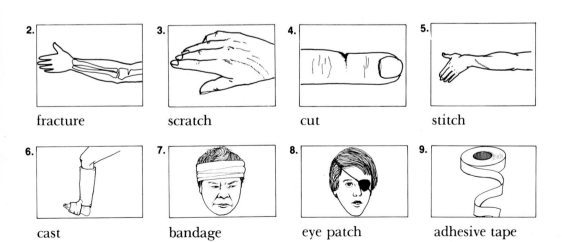

2. fracture	3. scratch	4. cut	5. stitch
6. cast	7. bandage	8. eye patch	9. adhesive tape

CONVERSATION 1A: An Accident

1.

A. Help, I can't get up.
B. I'll call an ambulance.

2.

B. Stay here and keep her comfortable.
C. Hurry!

3.

B. Operator, I'm calling about an accident.
D. Where are you?

4.

B. I am at the corner of Alameda Boulevard and Second Street.
D. We'll send an ambulance now.

5.

B. She was hit by a car.
E. Give me your name, address and phone number.

6.

A. Diane Grand, 12 Wilson Avenue, 641-7306.
E. The doctor will see you now.

CONVERSATION 1B: An Accident

7.

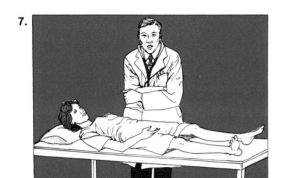

F. What happened?
A. I was hit by a car.

8.

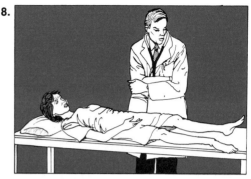

A. My leg hurts.
F. Can you move it?
A. No, I can't.

9.

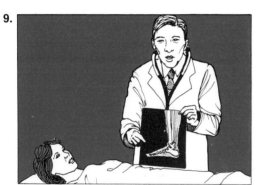

F. The x-ray shows a fractured ankle.
A. Does that mean it's broken?
F. Yes.

10.

F. We'll put it in a cast.
   Don't get it wet.
A. I won't.

11.

A. Will I be able to walk?
F. You'll need crutches.

12.

A. How long will I need the
   cast?
F. Six weeks.

CONVERSATION PLUS

Use the words in parentheses in each sentence below to make new sentences.

1. Help, I can't **get up**. (*stand up, move, turn, breathe*)
2. I'll call **an ambulance**. (*a doctor, a policeman, a friend, a neighbor, your family*)
3. We'll send an ambulance **now**. (*right away, right now, immediately, soon, at once*)
4. **She** was hit by a car. (*He, Diane, I*)
5. Can you **move** it? (*bend, raise, lower, turn*)
6. Will I be able to **walk**? (*run, jump, swim, sit*)
7. You'll need **crutches**. (*a stretcher, a cast, a sling, a wheelchair*)

WHAT'S RIGHT?

Make the *appropriate* choice. Choose a, b, or c for each number below.

1. Help, I can't get up.
   - ☐ a. Hurry!
   - ☐ b. I'm calling about an accident.
   - ☐ c. I'll call an ambulance.

2. Stay here and keep her comfortable.
   - ☐ a. Now.
   - ☐ b. Hurry!
   - ☐ c. Right away.

3. Operator, I'm calling about an accident.
  ☐ a. Where are you?
  ☐ b. How are you?
  ☐ c. Can you move it?

4. ☐ a. Does that mean it's broken?
  ☐ b. Where are you?
  ☐ c. What happened?

            I was hit by a car.

5. ☐ a. How long will I need the cast?
  ☐ b. Can you move it?
  ☐ c. What happened?

            No, I can't.

6. Don't get it wet.
  ☐ a. Hurry!
  ☐ b. Yes.
  ☐ c. I won't.

7. ☐ a. How long will I need the cast?
  ☐ b. Does that mean it's broken?
  ☐ c. Will I be able to walk?

            Six weeks.

YOUR TURN

Fill in each blank with an *appropriate* question or answer.

1. A. Help, I can't get up.
   B. _____

2. A. Operator, I'm calling about an accident.
   B. _____

3. A. What happened?
   B. _____

4. A. _____
   B. No, I can't.

5. A. Does that mean it's broken?
   B. _____

6. A. _____
   B. I won't.

7. A. _____
   B. Six weeks.

ROLE PLAY

1. Your friend is in an accident. She asks you for help and you help her. You also speak to the Emergency Operator and the nurse at the hospital.

   Your friend: _____

   You: _____

   You: _____

   Operator: _____

   You: _____

   Operator: _____

   You: _____

   Nurse: _____

2. You were in an accident. The doctor asks you what happened. You tell him and he helps you.

   Doctor: _____

   You: _____

   Doctor: _____

   You: _____

   Doctor: _____

   You: _____

WORD PLAY

Choose the word that is *inappropriate* in each group.

1. brain, heart, kidney, fracture
2. stomach, cut, intestine, liver
3. heart, bandage, eye patch, adhesive tape
4. walker, wheelchair, scratch, cane
5. paramedic, mask, surgeon, nurse
6. wound, crutch, scratch, cut
7. sling, bandage, eye patch, receptionist

READING 1: If There Is an Accident

If there is an accident, call the Emergency Number in your city. If you don't know this number, dial "O" for "Operator." The Operator will help you.

Don't move the patient. If the patient is bleeding, use pressure on the wound until help arrives. Keep him warm and calm. Wait with him until the ambulance comes.

If you study First Aid, you will know what to do in any emergency. The Red Cross gives classes in First Aid. The number is in the *White Pages* of your telephone book. It is a good idea to be prepared for an emergency. People say, "An ounce of prevention is worth a pound of cure."

Just the Facts

Tell whether the following statements are true or false.

1. If there's an accident, call the Emergency Number in your city.

2. Move the patient to a more comfortable position.

3. Apply ice to the wound.

4. If the patient is bleeding, use pressure on the wound.

5. The Salvation Army gives many courses in First Aid.

6. The telephone number for the Red Cross is in the *Yellow Pages.*

7. It is a good idea to be prepared for an emergency.

8. "An ounce of prevention is worth a pound of cure."

READING 2: The Emergency Room

If you are hurt, go to the Emergency Room at the nearest hospital. If it is not serious, you may have to wait. If you have medical insurance, bring the cards and forms with you. Bring a friend to help you.

There are many types of emergencies. The Emergency Room can take care of injuries that are serious or not serious. A cut or scratch is not serious. A fracture or a lot of bleeding can be serious. The doctors and nurses are prepared for any emergency, 24 hours a day. There is emergency equipment ready all of the time. The doctor can tell you if the injury is serious.

Catching On

Answer the following questions.

1. Where should you go if you are hurt?
2. What should you bring with you to the Emergency Room?
3. What type of injuries are not serious?
4. What type of injuries can be serious?
5. When is the emergency equipment ready?
6. Who can tell you if the injury is serious?

What Do You Think?

Answer the following questions.

1. Were you ever in an accident? Tell the class what happened.
2. Were you ever in an Emergency Room? Tell the class what happened.
3. Would you go to an Emergency Room if you had a cut?
4. Would you like to study First Aid?
5. "An ounce of prevention is worth a pound of cure" is a famous proverb. What does it mean? Do you think it is true?
6. What happens in an emergency in your country?

TALK IT OVER

Work with another student in the class. Each person asks the other the information on the hospital admission form below.

Joseph M. Ford General Hospital

Hospital Admission Form

Last Name	First Name	Initial

Address	Telephone

Doctor's Name	Complaint*

Name of Insurance Company	Policy Number

Name of Nearest Relative	Relationship

Address	Telephone

---

*complaint — problem

DO IT

A. Look up the names and telephone numbers of three hospitals in your city. Look under "Hospitals" in the *Yellow Pages* of the telephone book.

1. _____
   Hospital   Address   Telephone

2. _____
   Hospital   Address   Telephone

3. _____
   Hospital   Address   Telephone

B. Look up the Emergency Telephone Number in your city. Call Information or look in the *Yellow Pages* or the *White Pages* of the telephone book.

_____
Emergency Telephone Number

C. Look up the telephone number of two drugstores near you. Use the *Yellow Pages* of the telephone book.

1. _____
   Drugstore   Address   Telephone

2. _____
   Drugstore   Address   Telephone

FOR YOUR INFORMATION

A. To be prepared for an emergency:

  1. Always carry identification with you. Include your name and address. Include the name of a person to call.
  2. Know the name of your doctor and his telephone number.
  3. Know about any special health problems that you have.
  4. Know the name of any medicine that you are taking.
  5. Know your blood type.
  6. If you are an epileptic, diabetic, or allergic to any medicine, wear a special identification bracelet at all times. You can get this at your drugstore.

B. Copy the form below. Fill it out and carry it with you at all times.

IDENTIFICATION FORM

Name   Address   Telephone

Doctor's Name   Telephone

In an emergency call: Name   Telephone

My blood type is: _____

I am allergic to: _____

THE DENTIST

The Dentist

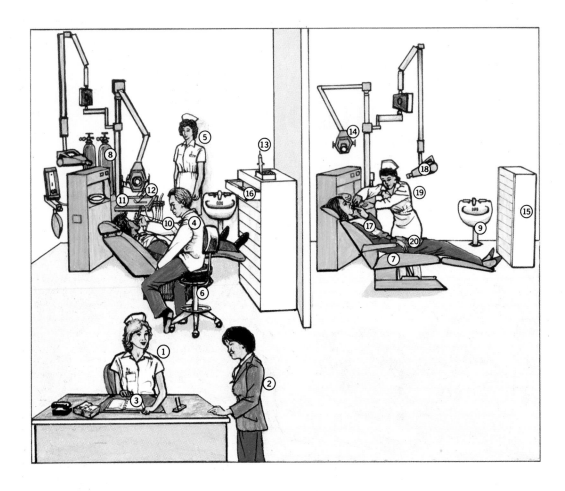

1. secretary
2. patient
3. appointment book
4. dentist
5. assistant
6. stool
7. dental chair
8. gas
9. sink
10. drill
11. tray
12. mirror
13. Novocaine
14. light
15. cabinet
16. drawer
17. towel
18. x-ray machine
19. hygienist
20. lead apron

PRACTICE WITH PICTURES

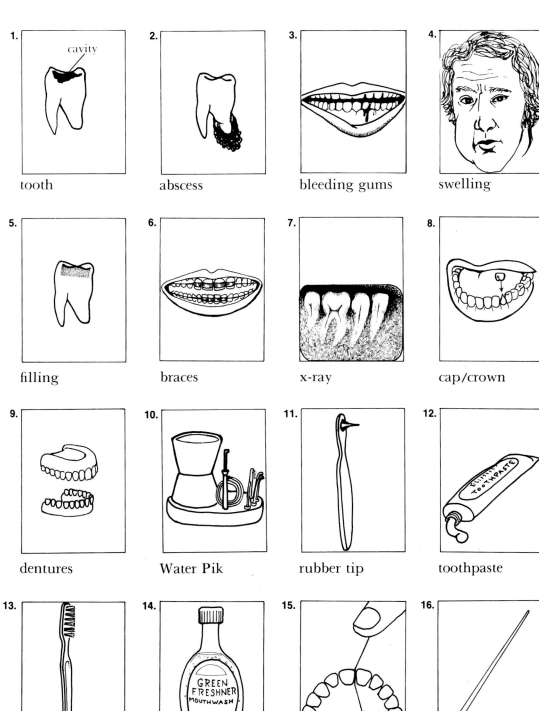

1. tooth

2. abscess

3. bleeding gums

4. swelling

5. filling

6. braces

7. x-ray

8. cap/crown

9. dentures

10. Water Pik

11. rubber tip

12. toothpaste

13. toothbrush

14. mouthwash

15. dental floss

16. toothpick

CONVERSATION 1A: A Toothache

A. Good morning, can I help you?
B. Yes, my name is Mrs. Chiu. I have a 10 o'clock appointment.

A. Please sit down. The doctor will see you soon.
B. Thank you.

A. Dr. Brenner, this is Mrs. Chiu.
C. Hello, Mrs. Chiu. Please come with me.

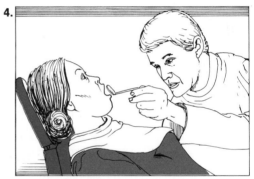

C. What's the problem?
B. I have a toothache.

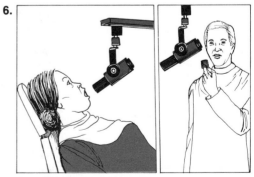

C. How long have you had it?
B. Four days.

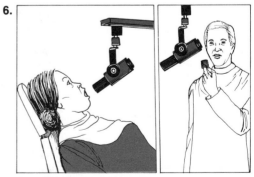

C. I'll take an x-ray. You have a cavity, but I can fill it.
B. Good.

CONVERSATION 1B: A Toothache

7.

C. I'll give you some Novocaine first.
B. Okay.

8.

B. Will it hurt?
C. No, it won't hurt.

9.

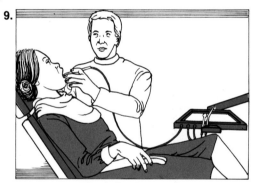

C. Now I can drill the tooth. Do you feel any pain?
B. No, I don't.

10.

C. There, it's filled.
B. Thanks, Doctor.

11.

B. When can I eat?
C. In two hours.

12.

C. You need an appointment with the hygienist to clean your teeth.
B. Fine.

CONVERSATION PLUS

Use the words in parentheses in each sentence below to make new sentences.

1. **I** have an appointment. (*We, They, You*)
2. The doctor will see you **soon**. (*now, in an hour, in ten minutes, right away*)
3. **Hello**, Mrs. Chiu. (*Hi, Good morning, Good afternoon*)
4. What's the **problem**? (*matter, trouble*)
5. I have **a toothache**. (*a pain, a swelling, a cavity, an abscess*)
6. You need **an appointment**. (*an x-ray, a filling, a cap, dentures*)

WHAT'S RIGHT?

Make the *appropriate* choice. Choose a, b, or c for each number below.

1. Good morning, can I help you?
   - ☐ a. Yes, my name is Mrs. Chiu.
   - ☐ b. Dr. Brenner, this is Mrs. Chiu.
   - ☐ c. Thanks, Doctor.

2. Please sit down.
   - ☐ a. Thank you.
   - ☐ b. Hello.
   - ☐ c. In two hours.

3. Dr. Brenner, this is Mrs. Chiu.
    ☐ a. Thanks, Doctor.
    ☐ b. Good.
    ☐ c. Hello, Mrs. Chiu.

4. What's the problem?
    ☐ a. I can fill it.
    ☐ b. I have a toothache.
    ☐ c. Four days.

5. Will it hurt?
    ☐ a. No, I don't.
    ☐ b. Okay.
    ☐ c. No, it won't.

6. When can I eat?
    ☐ a. In two hours.
    ☐ b. Fine.
    ☐ c. Four days.

7. ☐ a. What's the problem?
   ☐ b. Do you feel any pain?
   ☐ c. Will it hurt?
                   No, I don't.

8. ☐ a. How long have you had it?
   ☐ b. Will it hurt?
   ☐ c. Can I help you?
                   Four days.

YOUR TURN

Fill in each blank with an *appropriate* question or answer.

1. A. Good morning, can I help you?
   B. _____

2. A. What's the problem?
   B. _____

3. A. How long have you had it?
   B. _____

4. A. I'll give you some Novocaine first.
   B. _____

5. A. _____
   B. No, it won't.

6. A. Do you feel any pain?
   B. _____

7. A. _____
   B. In two hours.

ROLE PLAY

1. You have a toothache and go to the dentist. You tell the dentist the problem and the dentist helps you.

   You: _____

   Dentist: _____

   You: _____

   Dentist: _____

   You: _____

   Dentist: _____

2. You have a swelling. You call the dentist's office for an appointment and tell the secretary what the trouble is. The secretary tells you what to do.

   You: _____

   Secretary: _____

   You: _____

   Secretary: _____

   You: _____

   Secretary: _____

WORD PLAY

Complete the sentences below with the *appropriate* word from the Word List. You can use some words in more than one sentence.

Sentences

a. I have _____.

b. Mr. Delaney has _____.

c. I need _____.

d. Sylvia needs _____.

e. Use _____ every day.

f. Go to _____.

Word List

1. a toothbrush
2. a filling
3. a cavity
4. an abscess
5. a toothpick
6. a cap/a crown
7. bleeding gums
8. dental floss

9. an appointment
10. the dentist
11. the hospital
12. the clinic
13. mouthwash
14. toothpaste
15. the Emergency Room

READING 1: Care of Your Teeth

Brush your teeth after every meal. If you can't brush, rinse* with mouthwash or plain water. If you have food between your teeth, use a toothpick. Use dental floss every day. A Water Pik and a rubber tip are two other ways you can keep your teeth and gums clean and healthy. Ask your dentist what is best for you. You should see your dentist twice a year for a check-up*.

*rinse — wash
*check-up — examination

Catching On

Answer the following questions.

1. Name two ways to keep your teeth clean.
2. What should you do if you have food between your teeth?
3. How often should you brush your teeth?
4. How often should you use dental floss?
5. If you can't brush your teeth, what should you do?
6. How often should you see your dentist?

READING 2: Dental Problems

If you have a toothache, take two aspirin every four hours. Do not put aspirin on your gums. Go to a dentist as soon as possible. You can go to a dental clinic or an Emergency Room at the nearest hospital.

   If you have an abscess, you may have a swelling. First, rinse your mouth with a half-teaspoon of salt in a full glass of hot water. Then put ice in a towel and put it on the swelling. Leave it there for ten minutes. Then, take it off and leave it off for ten minutes. Repeat this often and see your dentist as soon as you can.

Just the Facts

Tell whether the following statements are true or false.

1. If you have a swelling, rinse your mouth with a half-teaspoon of salt in a full
   · glass of hot water.
2. You can go to a dental clinic or an Emergency Room at the nearest hospital.
3. If you have a toothache, put aspirin on your gums.
4. If you have an abscess, use a toothpick.
5. If you have a toothache, take two aspirin every four hours.
6. See your dentist as soon as you can.

What Do You Think?

Answer the following questions.

1. What do you do when you have a toothache?
2. If you have a cavity, what do you do?
3. If you have an abscess, what do you do?
4. Do you like to go to the dentist?
5. How often do you go to the dentist?
6. Why do you think it's important to keep your teeth clean?
7. Would you like to be a dentist?

TALK IT OVER

Fill out the following questionnaire for three people. When you have the information, share it with the class.

Questions	1	2	3
1. Which toothpaste do you use?			
2. How often do you go to the dentist?			
3. Did you ever have a toothache?			
4. Do you use a toothpick?			
5. Do you use dental floss?			

DO IT

A. Using the list below, write the addresses and phone numbers of the following dentists (DDS means dentist. DMD also means dentist).

	Address	Phone Number
1. Robert E. Brenner, DDS	_____	_____
2. Frank Chan, DMD	_____	_____
3. George Dressin, DDS	_____	_____

Bastos, Juan, DDS	30 Washington St.	796-4270
Brenner, Robert E., DDS	42 Fifth Ave.	431-4962
Bricker, Irving, DDS	47 Fourth Ave.	796-2444
Brinker, Joseph, DDS	62 Hawthorne St.	632-9416
Brody, Henry, DDS	24 Independence Rd.	731-8452
Brody, Murray, DDS	16 Hudson St.	131-6215
Chan, Frank, DMD	15 Houston St.	757-8551
Chang, Vivien, DDS	142 Ames Pl.	742-9261
Davis, Bruce, DDS	169 College Rd.	432-9998
Della Rocca, Vincent, DDS	2 Fieldston Rd.	664-7223
Dressin, George, DDS	14 180th St.	514-6798

B. Go to the *Yellow Pages* of the telephone book and write the names, addresses, and phone numbers of two dentists near your school.

Name	Address	Phone Number
1. _____	_____	_____
2. _____	_____	_____

FOR YOUR INFORMATION

A. To find a dentist:

1. Ask your neighbor or a friend.
2. Call the Dental Society of the state. You can find this number in the *White Pages* of the telephone book.
3. Look for dentists in the *Yellow Pages* of the telephone book.
4. You can go to the clinic or Emergency Room at the nearest hospital.

B. Forms you may need:

1. Dental insurance helps pay your dentist. Some companies have dental insurance for their employees. Ask your employer for this form.
2. Medicaid pays the dentist for some people. Call your local Welfare Office for this form.

HOUSING

Housing

1. apartment house
2. house
3. walk
4. lawn
5. garage
6. driveway
7. floor plan
8. entrance hall/entry
9. living room
10. window
11. window sill
12. radiator
13. kitchen
14. sink
15. faucet
16. stove
17. oven
18. burner
19. refrigerator
20. freezer
21. bedroom
22. bathroom
23. toilet
24. shower
25. shower curtain
26. bathtub

PRACTICE WITH PICTURES

1. door
2. doormat
3. door bell
4. lock
5. key
6. dishwasher
7. washing machine
8. dryer
9. lease
10. neighbor
11. janitor
12. view
13. stairway
14. closet
15. security guard
16. roof

CONVERSATION 1A: Looking for an Apartment

1.

A. Riverdale Realty, John Brown speaking.
B. Hello, my name is Kenji Endo.

2.

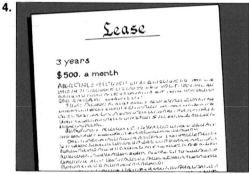

B. I'm calling about the ad.
A. Which one?
B. The three-room apartment.

3.

B. How much is the rent?
A. $500.00 a month plus a $1000.00 deposit.

4.

B. Do I have to sign a lease?
A. Yes, you do. It's a three-year lease.

5.

B. When can I see it?
A. You can see it today at two o'clock.

6.

A. I'll meet you at the apartment.
B. That's fine, thanks.

CONVERSATION 1B: Looking at the Apartment

7.

A. This is the living room.
B. It's very large.

8.

A. The kitchen has a new sink and stove.
B. Where's the refrigerator?
A. It's over there.

9.

A. The bedroom has a beautiful river view.
B. Yes, it does.

10.

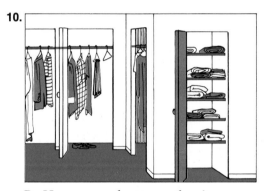

B. How many closets are there?
A. Three clothes closets and a linen closet.

11.

A. The bathroom is very modern.
B. Does it have a shower and a bathtub?
A. Yes, it does.

12.

B. I like it. I'll take it.
A. Good. You can sign the lease in my office.

CONVERSATION PLUS

Use the words in parentheses in each sentence below to make new sentences.

1. **Do I have to** sign a lease? (*Can I, Should I, Must I*)
2. When can I **see** it? (*buy, sell, have*)
3. You can see it **today** at two o'clock. (*tomorrow, Monday, Tuesday, Wednesday, Thursday, Friday, Saturday, Sunday*)
4. I'll meet you **at the apartment**. (*on the street, at the corner, in front of the building, at the entrance*)
5. This is the **living room**. (*bedroom, kitchen, bathroom, foyer*)
6. Where's the **refrigerator**? (*stove, sink, closet, shower*)
7. Does it have a **shower**? (*view, bathtub, refrigerator, stove*)

WHAT'S RIGHT?

Make the *appropriate* choice. Choose a, b, or c for each number below.

1. Riverdale Realty, John Brown speaking.

   ☐ a. The three-room apartment.
   ☐ b. Hello, my name is Kenji Endo.
   ☐ c. It's a three-year lease.

2. I'm calling about the ad.

   ☐ a. Hello, my name is Kenji Endo.
   ☐ b. Which one?
   ☐ c. $500.00 a month.

3. How much is the rent?

☐ a. You can see it today
at two o'clock.

☐ b. $1000.00 deposit.

☐ c. $500.00 a month.

4. ☐ a. How much is the rent?

☐ b. When can I see it?

☐ c. Do I have to sign a lease?

Yes, you do.

5. ☐ a. Which one?

☐ b. When can I see it?

☐ c. Do I have to sign a lease?

You can see it today
at two o'clock.

6. I'll meet you at the apartment.

☐ a. Yes, you do.

☐ b. It's a three-year lease.

☐ c. That's fine, thanks.

7. Where is the refrigerator?

☐ a. Yes, it does.

☐ b. It has a new sink and stove.

☐ c. It's over there.

8. Does it have a shower and a
bathtub?

☐ a. Yes, you do.

☐ b. Yes, it does.

☐ c. I like it. I'll take it.

YOUR TURN

Fill in each blank with an *appropriate* question or answer.

1. A. Riverdale Realty, John Brown speaking.
   B. _____

2. A. I'm calling about the ad.
   B. _____

3. A. How much is the rent?
   B. _____

4. A. Do I have to sign a lease?
   B. _____

5. A. When can I see it?
   B. _____

6. A. Where's the refrigerator?
   B. _____

7. A. _____
   B. Three clothes closets and a linen closet.

8. A. Does it have a shower and a bathtub?
   B. _____

ROLE PLAY

1. You are looking for an apartment. You see an ad in the paper. You call the real estate agent* and ask about the apartment. The agent answers your questions.

   You: _____

   Agent: _____

   You: _____

   Agent: _____

   You: _____

   Agent: _____

2. The agent shows you the apartment and tells you about it.

   Agent: _____

   You: _____

   Agent: _____

   You: _____

   Agent: _____

   You: _____

*real estate agent — a person who buys, sells, and rents different kinds of housing

WORD PLAY

Complete the sentences below with the *appropriate* word from the Word List. You can use some words in more than one sentence.

Sentences

a. Does it have a _____?

b. Where's the _____?

c. How much is the _____?

d. This is the _____.

e. You can see it _____.

Word List

1. bathtub
2. view
3. refrigerator
4. neighborhood
5. shower
6. security guard
7. rent

8. stove
9. Monday
10. key
11. stairway
12. Wednesday
13. lease
14. Saturday

READING: Types of Housing

There are many types of housing: co-ops,* condominiums, rentals, and private housing.

A Co-op: In a co-op, the tenants* own the building. They manage* the building. They are responsible for any repairs. No one can buy or sell an apartment without permission from the others.

A Condominium: In a condominium, the tenant owns his apartment. A company manages the building. The company is responsible for any repairs. A tenant can buy or sell his apartment without permission from anyone.

Rental: In a rental apartment house, the tenant pays rent* to a landlord* each month. The tenant does not own the apartment or the building. The landlord is responsible for repairs. The tenant signs a lease. This is an agreement between the tenant and the landlord. The lease states* the amount of rent the tenant must pay. There are one-, two-, and three-year leases.

A Private House: Owning a private house means you are the landlord and the tenant. You are responsible for everything. You can borrow money from the bank to buy the house. The agreement with the bank is called a mortgage.

*co-op — cooperative apartment house
*tenant — person who lives in the apartment
*manage — control
*landlord — owner of property
*rent — amount of money paid each month
*states — says or tells

Just the Facts

Tell whether the following statements are true or false.

1. In a co-op, the tenants own the building.
2. In a condominium, the landlord owns the building.
3. In a rental apartment house, the tenant owns the apartment.
4. Owning a private house means you are the tenant and the landlord.
5. In a co-op, anyone can buy or sell the apartment.
6. In a condominium, anyone can buy or sell the apartment.

Catching On

Answer the following questions.

1. Who manages the building in a co-op?
2. Who is responsible for repairs in a condominium?
3. Who is responsible for repairs in a co-op?
4. Who manages a condominium?
5. Who is responsible for repairs in a private house?
6. Who is responsible for repairs in a rental apartment house?

What Do You Think?

Answer the following questions.

1. Would you like to live in a co-op? Tell why or why not.
2. Would you like to live in a condominium? Tell why or why not.
3. Would you like to live in a rental apartment house? Tell why or why not.
4. Would you like to own your own house? Tell why or why not.

TALK IT OVER

Talk with other students in groups. Each group discusses which of the following types of housing they think is best. One person from each group reports to the class.

1.
Condominium

Living room; kitchen with dishwasher, stove, and refrigerator; 2 bedrooms; 1 bathroom; river view. $50,000.

2.
Co-op

Living room; 1 bedroom; kitchen with stove, refrigerator, and washer and dryer; 1 bathroom; wooded area. $35,000.

3.
Private House

Living room; kitchen with stove, refrigerator, and dishwasher; 2 bathrooms; 3 bedrooms; garage; lawn. $97,000.

4.
Rental Apartment

Living room; 2 bedrooms; 2 bathrooms; kitchen with new stove and refrigerator; mountain view; 3-year lease. $600 a month.

DO IT

A. Study the list of abbreviations below. These are the short forms of words usually found in ads for housing.

1. rm=room
2. rms=rooms
3. apt=apartment
4. apts=apartments
5. bdrm=bedroom
6. lvrm=living room
7. pvt hse=private house
8. mod=modern
9. lge=large
10. riv vu=river view
11. bth=bathroom
12. lux bldg=luxury building
13. excel cond=excellent condition
14. mrtg = mortgage
15. kit=kitchen
16. avail immed=available immediately
17. refrg=refrigerator
18. loc=location
19. condo=condominium
20. wash/dry=washer and dryer
21. co-op=co-operative apartment house

DO IT

B. Look at the ads below. They use the abbreviations. Write the long form of the words for each ad below.

Example:

Ad 1

3 rms; riv vu;
lux bldg

Long Form

3 rooms; river view;
luxury building

Ad 2

Long Form

> Pvt hse; 3 bdrms;
>
> 2 bths; excel cond;
>
> good mrtg

Ad 3

Long Form

> Mod apt; 4 rms;
>
> lge lvrm;
>
> 1 bth; new refrg;
>
> good loc

Ad 4

Long Form

> Condo; lux bldg;
>
> 2 bdrms; mod kit;
>
> avail immed; riv vu

Ad 5

Long Form

> Co-op; 6 rms;
>
> 2 bths; excel cond;
>
> new bldg; mod kit;
>
> wash/dry; new refrg;
>
> excel loc

FOR YOUR INFORMATION

A. Finding housing:

1. To find an apartment or a house look in the *Real Estate* section of the newspaper. Most ads are on Saturdays and Sundays.
2. Look in the *Yellow Pages* of the telephone book under "Real Estate Agents." Call a Real Estate agent near you for help.
3. Real Estate agents charge you for finding housing. They usually charge one month's rent for finding a rental apartment. They usually charge a percentage* of the selling price for finding a co-op, condo, or private house.
4. Go to apartment buildings and ask the janitor if an apartment is available*.
5. Call the housing office or the foreign student advisor's office at the local university.
6. Ask your friends for help.

B. Complaints:

1. A tenant has a right to complain about the following problems:
   a. leaks
   b. not enough heat
   c. broken refrigerators, stoves, sinks, toilets
   d. poor condition of the building
2. If you have a complaint speak to your landlord.
3. If your landlord does not help, call the appropriate office under your city government. This is listed in the *White Pages* of your telephone book. If you can't find the telephone number, ask the operator for information.

*percentage — part of
*available — empty

FIRE AND ROBBERY

Fire and Robbery

A. Fire
1. fireman
2. fire truck
3. hydrant
4. ladder
5. fire
6. smoke
7. hose
8. net
9. megaphone/bullhorn
10. fire escape

B. Robbery
1. policeman/cop
2. thief
3. police car
4. witness
5. siren
6. flasher/emergency light
7. victim
8. knife
9. gun
10. nightstick
11. handbag/purse

PRACTICE WITH PICTURES

1.
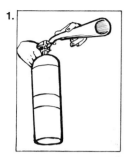
fire extinguisher

2.
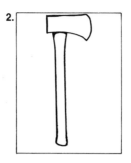
axe

3.
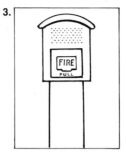
fire alarm box

4.

burn

5.
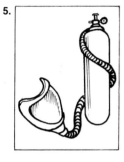
oxygen

6.

smoke detector

7.

fingerprint

8.

walkie-talkie

9.

police dog

10.

line-up

11.
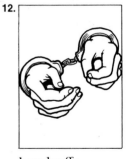
siren

12.

handcuffs

13.
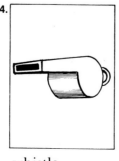
badge

14.

whistle

15.

bullet

16.

uniform

CONVERSATION 1: A Fire in the Apartment

1.

A. Do you hear that?
B. What?

2.

A. The smoke detector is ringing.
B. Where?

3.

A. I think it's in the kitchen.
B. Let's look.

4.

A. Do you smell smoke?
B. Yes, I do.

5.

B. Oh! The stove is on fire.
A. Get the fire extinguisher.

6.

B. Be calm, it's under control.
A. Yes, but dinner is ruined.

CONVERSATION 2: A Burglary

1.

A. Don't move. This is a hold-up.
B. Please don't hurt us.

2.

A. Be quiet and you won't get hurt.
C. What do you want?

3.

A. Give me all your money.
B. Here.
C. Here's mine.

4.

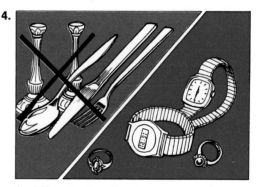

A. Where's the silver?
C. We don't have any.
A. Give me your rings and your watches.

5.

A. I'm going now. Don't call the police.
B. Okay.

6.

C. I'm going to call the police.
B. Do you think we should?
C. I think we must.

CONVERSATION PLUS

Use the words in parentheses in each sentence below to make new sentences.

1. I think it's the **kitchen**. (*bedroom, living room, bathroom, hall*)
2. Do you smell **smoke**? (*perfume, food, flowers, gas*)
3. The **stove** is on fire. (*house, garage, car, building*)
4. Don't **move**. (*run, jump, talk, scream*)
5. Please don't **hurt** us. (*hit, kill, beat, shoot*)
6. Give me your **rings**. (*watches, money, jewelry, silver*)
7. Do you think **we** should? (*you, I, she, he, they*)
8. I think **we** must. (*you, I, she, he, they*)

WHAT'S RIGHT?

Make the *appropriate* choice. Choose a, b, or c for each number below.

1. Do you smell smoke?

   ☐ a. The smoke detector is
      ringing.
   ☐ b. Yes, I do.
   ☐ c. It's under control.

2. The stove is on fire.

   ☐ a. Yes, but dinner is ruined.
   ☐ b. Yes, I do.
   ☐ c. Get the fire extinguisher.

3. This is a hold-up.

☐ a. Please don't hurt us.
☐ b. We don't have any.
☐ c. I think we must.

4. ☐ a. Don't move.
   ☐ b. Give me all your money.
   ☐ c. Be quiet and you won't get hurt.

Here.

5. ☐ a. What do you want?
   ☐ b. This is a hold-up.
   ☐ c. Where's the silver?

We don't have any.

6. Do you think we should?

☐ a. Please don't hurt us.
☐ b. I think we must.
☐ c. I'm going to call
    the police.

YOUR TURN

Fill in each blank with an *appropriate* question or answer.

1. A. Do you hear that?

   B. _____

2. A. The smoke detector is ringing.

   B. _____

3. A. Do you smell smoke?

   B. _____

4. A. Oh! The stove is on fire.

   B. _____

5. A. This is a hold-up.

   B. _____

6. A. _____

   B. We don't have any.

7. A. _____

   B. I think we must.

ROLE PLAY

1. There's a small fire in your apartment. You hear the smoke detector and you have a fire extinguisher. You and your roommate put out the fire.

   You:_____

   Roommate:_____

   You:_____

   Roommate:_____

   You:_____

   Roommate:_____

2. You are the victim of a crime. A burglar shows you his gun and robs your apartment.

   Burglar:_____

   You:_____

   Burglar:_____

   You:_____

   Burglar:_____

   You:_____

WORD PLAY

Choose the word that is *inappropriate* in each group.

1. thief, victim, witness, handcuffs
2. fire, net, hose, ladder
3. megaphone, siren, whistle, knife
4. knife, purse, nightstick, gun
5. fireman, fire, fire truck, policeman
6. hydrant, hose, megaphone, water
7. net, policeman, police car, siren

READING 1: In Case of Fire

You can put out small fires with a fire extinguisher. Everyone should have a fire extinguisher and a smoke detector in their house. You can buy these in a department store. They are not expensive and can save your life.

In large fires, you should call the Fire Department to put out the fire. It is important to get everyone out of the house as quickly as possible. Stay calm.

Just the Facts

Tell whether the following statements are true or false.

1. Everyone should have a fire in their house.
2. You can buy a fire extinguisher and a smoke detector in a department store.
3. A smoke detector is very expensive.
4. You can put out large fires with a fire extinguisher.
5. It is important to get everyone out of a house as quickly as possible.
6. Stay calm.

READING 2: What To Do If You Are a Crime Victim

If someone attacks you, do not resist*. Try to remain calm. Your attacker is probably nervous*. If you resist, he may hurt you. Give him what he asks for. Your life is more important than your money.

Try to remember what the attacker looks like. It's important to be able to describe the attacker to the police. You should report any crime to the police. It's their job to help you.

*resist — fight back
*nervous — afraid

Just the Facts

Tell whether the following statements are true or false.

1. If someone attacks you, fight back.
2. Don't give him your money.
3. Try to remember what the attacker looks like.
4. You should report any crime to the police.

What Do You Think?

Answer the following questions.

1. Should you have a fire extinguisher and smoke detector in your house? Tell why or why not.
2. Tell what you would do if you had a fire in your house.
3. Tell what you would do if someone attacked you.
4. What do the police do with an attacker in your country?

TALK IT OVER

Fill out the following questionnaire for three people. When you have the information, share it with the class.

Questions	People		
	1	2	3
1. Name two things you would take with you if there was a fire in your apartment.			
2. In a fire, would you jump into a net from the fourth floor?			
3. In a fire, would you jump from the second floor without a net?			
4. Do you have a fire extinguisher in your apartment?			
5. Do you have a smoke detector in your apartment?			
6. Would you resist an attacker?			
7. Would you call the police about a robbery?			

DO IT

Look up the telephone numbers you may need in an emergency. Look in the front part of either the *White* or *Yellow Pages* of the telephone book. If you can't find them, ask the operator for help. Write the telephone numbers below.

1. Police: _____

2. Fire Department: _____

3. Burn Center: _____

4. Gas Leaks: _____

5. Gas and Electric Company: _____

6. Neighbor's Telephone Number: _____

FOR YOUR INFORMATION

A. Prevention of emergencies:

 1. Turn off burners on the stove when you don't use them.
 2. Don't put too many electric plugs in an outlet. The voltage in the United States is 110 volts. If your appliance* uses 220 volts you must have a converter.
 3. Do not touch outlets or appliances when your hands are wet.
 4. Do not put electrical appliances in water.

B. Suggestions for some emergencies:

 1. If you see a fire, use the nearest fire alarm box. These boxes are always red. Use the alarm box only for fire. A false alarm* can be dangerous.
 2. If your clothes are on fire, cover yourself in a rug or blanket.
 3. For minor burns, use cold water or cover the burn with a burn ointment.
 4. Keep a First Aid Kit in your house. You can make your own First Aid Kit or buy one in a drug store. A First Aid Kit should have the following things:
    a. bandage
    b. adhesive tape
    c. Band-Aids
    d. burn ointment
    e. antiseptic*

*appliance — *For example:* toaster, hair dryer, iron
*false alarm — using a fire alarm when there is no fire
*antiseptic — medicine used to prevent infection

JOBS

Jobs

1. receptionist
2. applicant
3. manager
4. file
5. filing cabinet
6. switchboard
7. switchboard operator
8. job counselor
9. card file
10. in-box
11. out-box
12. stapler
13. calculator
14. wastepaper basket
15. calendar
16. photocopier
17. typewriter

PRACTICE WITH PICTURES

1. salesman

2. cab driver

3. beautician

4. waiter/waitress

5. housekeeper

6. teacher

7. plumber

8. electrician

9. machinist

10. porter

11. construction worker

12. engineer

13. chef/cook

14. computer technician

15. pilot

16. tailor

CONVERSATION 1: Getting a Job

1.

A. I need a job.
B. What can you do?

2.

A. I'm a secretary.
B. Do you have any references?
A. Yes, I do.

3.

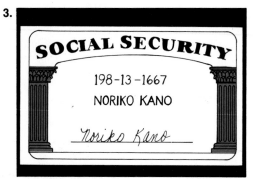

B. You need a Social Security card.
A. I have one.

4.

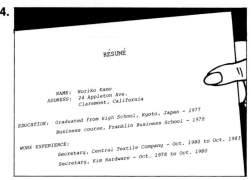

B. Can I see your résumé?
A. Here it is.

5.

B. There's a good job at the United Trading Company. The salary is $200.00 a week.
A. I'd like that.

6.

B. Fine, take this card to Mr. Kraft at the Company.
A. Thanks very much.

CONVERSATION 2: On the Job

1.

A. My name is Noriko Kano. I'm the new secretary.
B. Hi! I'm Joan Roberts.

2.

B. This is your desk and typewriter.
A. Good.

3.

A. Is there a dictating machine?
B. Yes, it's over there.

4.

A. What time do we start work?
B. Working hours are 9 to 5.

5.

B. There's a coffee break at 10:50.
A. When is lunch?

6.

B. Lunch is 12 to 1. Let's have lunch together.
A. Great!

CONVERSATION PLUS

Use the words in parentheses in each sentence below to make new sentences.

1. I **need** a job. (*want, have, am looking for*)
2. I'm a **secretary**. (*plumber, teacher, cook, computer technician*)
3. You need **a Social Security** card. (*a Green, an identification, a student*)
4. This is your **desk**. (*typewriter, phone, calculator, in-box*)
5. The salary is **$200.00 a week**. (*$800.00 a month, $800.00 monthly, $10,000.00 a year, $10,000.00 yearly*)
6. It's **over there**. (*over here, here, there*)
7. Working hours are **9 to 5**. (*8 to 4, 10 to 6, 8:30 to 5:30*)
8. When is **lunch**? (*dinner, breakfast, coffee break*)

WHAT'S RIGHT?

Make the *appropriate* choice. Choose a, b, or c for each number below.

1. Hello, my name is Noriko Kano.
   - ☐ a. Good.
   - ☐ b. Great.
   - ☐ c. Hi, I'm Joan Roberts.

2. ☐ a. When is lunch?   Yes, it's over there.
   - ☐ b. What time do we start work?
   - ☐ c. Is there a dictating machine?

3. ☐ a. I need a job.   Great.
   ☐ b. Let's have lunch together.
   ☐ c. You need a Social Security card.

4. Do you have any references?   ☐ a. Here it is.
                                        ☐ b. Yes, it's over there.
                                        ☐ c. Yes, I do.

5. The salary is $200.00 a week.   ☐ a. Here it is.
                                        ☐ b. I'm the new secretary.
                                        ☐ c. I'd like that.

6. Can I see your resumé?   ☐ a. Yes, I do.
                                        ☐ b. Good.
                                        ☐ c. Here it is.

YOUR TURN

Fill in each blank with an *appropriate* question or answer.

1. A. I need a job.
   B. _____

2. A. Do you have any references?
   B. _____

3. A. _____
   B. Here it is.

4. A. The salary is $200.00 a week.
   B. _____

5. A. My name is Noriko Kano. I'm the new secretary.
   B. _____

6. A. _____
   B. Yes, it's over there.

7. A. What time do we start work?
   B. _____

8. A. Let's have lunch together.
   B. _____

ROLE PLAY

1. You want a job. You go to an employment agency.

   You: _____

   Job Counselor: _____

   You: _____

   Job Counselor: _____

   You: _____

   Job Counselor: _____

2. It is your first day on the job. You meet a co-worker who helps you.

   Co-worker: _____

   You: _____

   Co-worker: _____

   You: _____

   Co-worker: _____

   You: _____

WORD PLAY

Choose the word that is *inappropriate* in each group.

1. receptionist, secretary, manager, typewriter
2. switchboard operator, card file, in-box, out-box
3. applicant, stapler, file, calculator
4. waitress, waiter, tailor, cook
5. chef, construction worker, engineer, electrician
6. photocopier, filing cabinet, switchboard, stapler
7. card file, calendar, file, filing cabinet

READING 1: Salary and Benefits

Most jobs offer a salary and benefits. A salary is money paid directly to you for your work.

Benefits are additional* things the company does for you. Vacation and sick leave* are benefits. Many companies also give health insurance and pensions. A pension is money you get when you retire*. Health insurance is money for your doctor and hospital bills. Some companies also give insurance to help pay your dentist bills.

*additional — extra
*sick leave — time off when you are sick
*retire — stop working at a certain age, usually over 60 years old

Just the Facts

Tell whether the following statements are true or false.

1. You get a salary after you stop working.
2. Dental insurance pays your hospital bill.
3. Most companies give health insurance.
4. A benefit is something extra the company gives.
5. You get a pension after you stop working.

What Do You Think?

Answer the following questions.

1. Why is a vacation important?
2. Are benefits necessary? Why?
3. Which is more important: health insurance or a vacation? Tell why.
4. Would you work for a company that didn't give sick leave? Tell why or why not.
5. Are there company benefits in your country?

READING 2: The Job Interview

The job interview is very important. It helps the employer decide whether* you are the right person for the job. Here are some suggestions for a successful interview.

1. Know the address and telephone number of the company.
2. Be on time for your appointment.
3. Women wear dresses or skirts and blouses; men wear jackets and ties.
4. Listen carefully to the questions and answer questions carefully.
5. Ask questions about the job.
6. Look directly at the interviewer.
7. Have your résumé with you.
8. Be confident*.

*whether — if
*confident — not afraid

Catching On

Answer the following questions.

1. Name two things that are important for a successful interview.
2. What should you bring to the interview?
3. What should men wear to an interview?
4. What should women wear to an interview?
5. Where should you look when you are being interviewed?

What Do You Think?

Answer the following questions.

1. Why is the interview important?
2. Would you ask questions at the interview?
3. Tell two questions you would ask.
4. Would you ask about the benefits?
5. Why is it important to be confident?

TALK IT OVER

Select a panel of four Job Counselors. Other students choose a job from the *Want Ads** below. They tell why they want that job. The panel decides which student gets which job.

Secretary

Secretary/Typist—experienced on dictating machine, good opportunity, $200./week. Telephone 564-2466. Apply to Personnel Manager, Mr. Kraft, at United Trading Company.

Construction Worker

No experience necessary. Work outdoors. Must be strong. Convenient location. Salary $325./week. Call Harding Construction, 762-3791.

Tailor

Five-day work week, experience necessary. Must be able to use a sewing machine. Apply to Scott Cleaners, 549-6327.

Sales

Sales Help—Westcott, Inc. has openings for full-time people in Shoe-, Sportswear- and Main Floor Departments. Good benefits, 35-hour work week. Apply to Personnel Department, 11 West 51st St., 5th floor.

Teacher

Teachers/Math, grades 6-8, (full-time: $20,000./year), (part-time: 2½ days, $10,000.). Must be certified. Send résumé to Mr. Davis at Merch School, 111 Lawson Avenue, Little Rock, Arkansas.

Waitress/Waiter

Waitress/Waiter—good restaurant, experienced, 8 p.m. to 3 a.m. Salary $150./week plus tips. Call Mr. Hendricks at Crosby Restaurant, 637-8451.

**Want Ads* — advertisements for jobs

DO IT: Write your own résumé using the model below.

RÉSUMÉ

Name: Lenore A. Schaefer

Address: 12 East Academy Street, Mesquite, Texas   76109

Phone: (817) 836-6744

Education: Del Camino High School (1974), Del Camino, Texas   78369

University of Texas (B.S. 1978), Arlington, Texas   76005

University of Texas (M.A. 1981), Dallas, Texas   75202

Experience: 1981 to Present - Teacher, Mesquite Elementary School, Mesquite, Texas   76109. Taught grades 1-3.

1980-1981 - Teacher, Navarro Elementary School, Dallas, Texas   75201. Taught grades 2-4.

1978-1979 - Teacher, San Patricio Elementary School, Madrid, Spain. Taught grades 1-5.

Interests: Languages, Reading, Tennis.

References: Dr. William Gonzales, Principal, Mesquite Elementary School, 299 Burgess Avenue, Mesquite, Texas   76109, (817) 836-1956.

Dr. Christopher Johnson, Chairman, Department of Foreign Languages and Linguistics, University of Texas, Dallas, Texas   75202, (817) 747-2536.

RÉSUMÉ

Name: _____

Address: _____

Phone: _____

_____

Education: _____

_____

_____

Experience: _____

_____

_____

_____

_____

_____

Interests: _____

References: _____

_____

_____

_____

_____

FOR YOUR INFORMATION

A. When you want a job:

1. Read the *Want Ads* in the newspaper.

2. Go to an employment agency.

3. Ask your friends for help.

4. Go to a company and ask if there is a job for you.

B. When you apply for a job:

1. Ask about salary and benefits.

2. Be sure that you get at least the minimum wage. This is the amount you *must* get by law.

3. Be sure you have a Social Security card.

4. Be sure you have a Green Card* if you are not a citizen.

C. When you leave your job or lose your job:

1. Ask about unemployment insurance.

2. Apply for Federal Assistance or Welfare if you have no money.

D. When you are hurt or get sick on the job:

1. Apply for Workmen's Compensation.

2. Ask your employer for the necessary forms.

E. When you need information:

1. Call the Welfare Office for welfare information.

2. Call the Unemployment Office for unemployment information.

3. Call the Department of Immigration for a Green Card. These offices are listed in the *White Pages* of your telephone book under the words "U.S. Government Offices."

*Green Card — alien registration card

BANKING

Banking

1. desk
2. table
3. pen
4. counter
5. bank manager
6. customer
7. guard
8. vault
9. safe deposit box
10. key
11. teller
12. T.V. camera
13. computer
14. banking machine/cash machine

PRACTICE WITH PICTURES

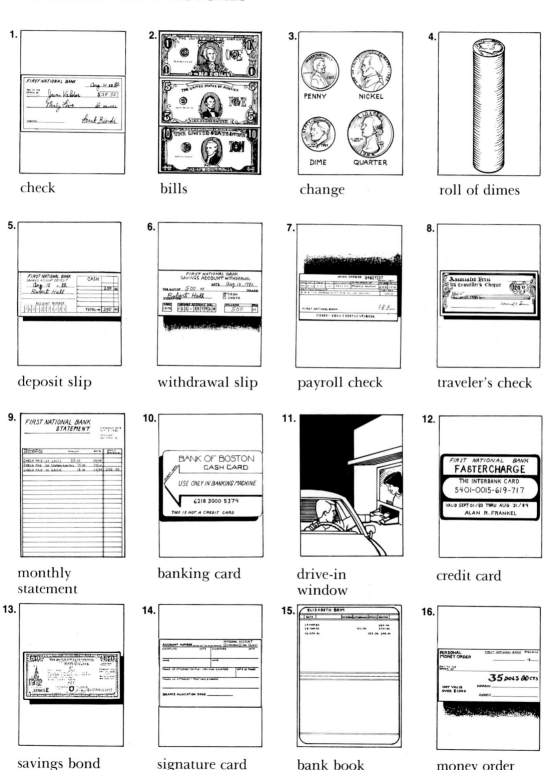

1. check

2. bills

3. change

4. roll of dimes

5. deposit slip

6. withdrawal slip

7. payroll check

8. traveler's check

9. monthly statement

10. banking card

11. drive-in window

12. credit card

13. savings bond

14. signature card

15. bank book

16. money order

CONVERSATION 1: Opening an Account

1.

A. My name is Juan Valdes. I want to open a bank account.

B. A checking account or a savings account?

2.

A. A checking account. I like to pay my bills by check.

B. Fine. Do you want a joint account or an individual account?

A. A joint account. Then my wife can use it, too.

3.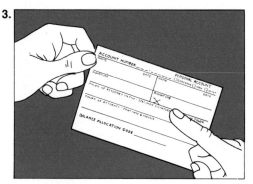

B. You sign here and your wife signs there.

A. Okay.

4.

B. How much money do you want to deposit?

A. $200.00.

5.

B. Fill out this deposit slip and give it to the teller with your money.

A. Can I write a check now?

6.

B. Yes, you can. Here's a checkbook.

A. Thank you very much.

CONVERSATION 2: Getting a Loan

1.

A. How can I get a loan?
B. Why do you want the money?
A. To buy a car.

2.

B. How much money do you need?
A. $2000.00.

3.

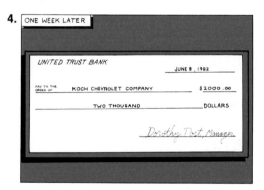

B. Please fill out this application.
A. When do I get the money?
B. In a week.

4.

B. Here's a bank check to the
   Koch Chevrolet Co. for $2000.00.
A. Thank you.

5.

B. The interest is eighteen
   percent. That's $360.00 a year.
A. That means I am paying a
   total of $2,360.00.

6.

A. Can I pay it monthly?
B. Yes. Your payments will
   be $196.67 each month.

CONVERSATION PLUS

Use the words in parentheses in each sentence below to make new sentences.

1. I want to open a **bank** account. (*checking, savings, joint, individual*)
2. How much money do you want to **deposit**? (*put in, take out, withdraw, transfer*)
3. I like to pay my bills by **check**. (*cash, money order*)
4. Why do you want the **money**? (*loan, cash, check, credit*)
5. Please **fill out** this application. (*make out, complete*)
6. You can get it in **a week**. (*a month, a year, a day, an hour*)
7. The interest is **18%***. (*5½%, 6%, 12%*)
8. Can I pay it **monthly**? (*yearly, annually, weekly, daily*)

*18% — eighteen percent

WHAT'S RIGHT?

Make the *appropriate* choice. Choose a, b, or c for each number below.

1. Do you want a joint account or an individual account?
   - ☐ a. A bank account.
   - ☐ b. A joint account.
   - ☐ c. A savings account.

2. How much money do you want to deposit?
   - ☐ a. $200.00.
   - ☐ b. 10%.
   - ☐ c. A monthly payment.

3. ☐ a. Do you want a checking account?   Yes, you can.
   - ☐ b. Do I sign here?
   - ☐ c. Can I write a check now?

4. Why do you want the money?

☐ a. Here's a bank check.
☐ b. To buy a car.
☐ c. $2,000.00.

5. When do I get the money?

☐ a. In a week.
☐ b. That's $360.00 a year.
☐ c. To buy a car.

6. ☐ a. Can I pay it weekly?
   ☐ b. Can I pay it monthly?
   ☐ c. Can I pay it annually?

Yes, your payments will
be $196.67 each month.

YOUR TURN

Fill in each blank with an *appropriate* question or answer.

1. A. I want to open a bank account.
   B. _____

2. A. Do you want a joint account or an individual account?
   B. _____

3. A. How much money do you want to deposit?
   B. _____

4. A. Why do you want a loan?

   B. _____

5. A. _____

   B. $2,000.00.

6. A. _____

   B. In a week.

7. A. _____

   B. Your payments will be $196.67 each month.

ROLE PLAY

1. You want to open an account. The Assistant Manager helps you.

   You: _____

   Assistant Manager: _____

   You: _____

   Assistant Manager: _____

   You: _____

   Assistant Manager: _____

2. You want a loan. The Bank Manager helps you.

You:_____

Bank Manager: _____

You:_____

Bank Manager: _____

You:_____

Bank Manager: _____

WORD PLAY

Choose the word that is *inappropriate* in each group.

1. checking account, deposit slip, savings account, joint account
2. deposit slip, withdrawal slip, monthly statement, bank guard
3. signature card, bills, change, roll of dimes
4. savings bond, customer, guard, teller
5. T.V. camera, computer, banking machine, traveler's check
6. payroll check, check, bills, traveler's check
7. teller, manager, assistant manager, bank book

READING 1: Automatic Banking

Automatic banking means using a machine. You can use the machine to get money from your account or to put money into your account. You must get a special banking card for the machine from the bank manager. You can use the machine any time, day or night, even when the bank is closed.

The machine can't do everything. It can't give you a loan. It can't open an account. It can't help you with special problems. You must talk to the manager for that.

Just the Facts

Tell whether the following statements are true or false.

1. You must get a special banking card for automatic banking.

2. You can get the card from the bank guard.

3. You can get money from the machine.

4. You can't use the machine to put money into your account.

5. You can use the machine at any time.

6. You can get a loan from the machine.

7. You must talk to the manager to open an account.

READING 2: How To Use a Banking Machine

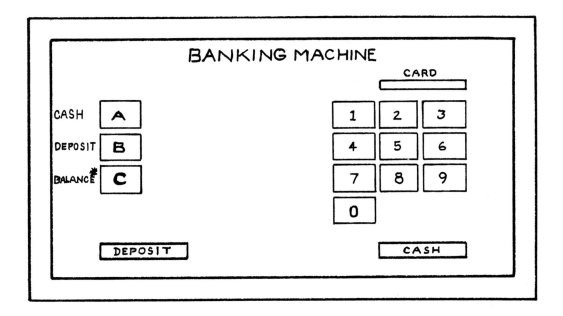

The buttons on the left tell the machine what to do.

You can get cash, make a deposit, or get your balance.

The buttons on the right tell the machine how much money you want to get or deposit.

If you press **A**, 1, 5, 0, 0, you will get $15.00 in cash.

If you press **A**, 1, 5, 2, 5, you will get $15.25 in cash.

If you press **A**, 1, 5, 0, 2, 5, you will get $150.25 in cash.

If you press **B**, 1, 5, 0, 0, you will deposit $15.00.

If you press **B**, 1, 5, 2, 5, you will deposit $15.25.

If you press **B**, 1, 5, 0, 2, 5, you will deposit $150.25.

If you press **C**, the machine tells you your balance.

*balance — amount of money in your account

Catching On

Make the correct choice. Choose a, b, c, or d for each number below.

1. If you press A, 1, 4, 5, 0, 0
   - ☐ a. You deposit $145.00
   - ☐ b. You get $145.00
   - ☐ c. You get your balance
   - ☐ d. You get $14.50

2. If you press B, 1, 3, 6, 0, 0
   - ☐ a. You deposit $136.00
   - ☐ b. You get $136.00
   - ☐ c. You get $1.36
   - ☐ d. You deposit $145.00

3. If you press C
   - ☐ a. You get $145.00
   - ☐ b. You get your balance
   - ☐ c. You deposit $13.60
   - ☐ d. You get $1450.00

4. If you press B, 1, 5, 0, 0
   - ☐ a. You deposit $150.00
   - ☐ b. You deposit $1.50
   - ☐ c. You deposit $15.00
   - ☐ d. You deposit $1,500.00

5. If you press A, 1, 4, 5, 6, 5
   - ☐ a. You get $145.65
   - ☐ b. You deposit $145.65
   - ☐ c. You get $14.65
   - ☐ d. You get your balance

What Do You Think?

Answer the following questions.

1. Would you like to use a banking machine? Tell why or why not.
2. Would you like to have a checking account? Tell why or why not.
3. Would you like to have a savings account? Tell why or why not.
4. Would you ever apply for a loan? Tell why or why not.
5. Would you like to work in a bank? Tell why or why not.
6. Tell about banks in your country.

TALK IT OVER

Talk with other students in groups. Each group discusses which of the following banks they think is best. One person from each group reports to the class.

United Bank

5% interest on savings
free checking accounts
free toaster
15% interest on loans

Certified Bank

5½% interest on savings
10¢ each check
free hair dryer
12% interest on loans

National Bank

6% interest on savings
You must keep $200.00 balance
    in your checking account
free T.V.
18% interest on loans

DO IT

A. Write a check below for each of the following bills.
1. Epps Department Store, $25.00 (for a lamp)
2. Central Telephone Company, $36.50 (phone bill)
3. Consolidated Gas & Light Company, $75.00 (gas and electric bill)

United National Bank   No. 564

_____ 19_____

Pay to the
order of _____ $_____

_____ DOLLARS

_____   _____
Memo   Signature

United National Bank   No. 565

_____ 19_____

Pay to the
order of _____ $_____

_____ DOLLARS

_____   _____
Memo   Signature

United National Bank   No. 566

_____ 19_____

Pay to the
order of _____ $_____

_____ DOLLARS

_____   _____
Memo   Signature

B. Now enter these checks in your checkbook. Balance the record below and subtract each amount from your balance.

Check Number	Date	Description of Transaction	Amount of Check		Amount of Deposit		Balance $700	00
563	9/11/82	John Brown Realty Co.	$200	00			$500	00

Check balance sheet addition.
Your final balance should be $363.50.

FOR YOUR INFORMATION

A. Banks are listed in the *Yellow Pages* of the telephone book.

B. Banks are "money stores." You should shop for the best bargain on interest rates and other services.

C. Safe deposit boxes are for keeping valuables* safe. Keep your birth certificate, your passport, and your will* in a safe deposit box.

D. You can get a loan from a Loan Company. These are listed in the *Yellow Pages* of the telephone book.

E. Check cashing services are listed in the *Yellow Pages* of the telephone book. A check cashing service sells money orders and food stamps, and cashes checks.

F. Do not pay more interest than the maximum* rate the law allows. Interest rates change. Ask the bank for the current maximum interest rate.

G. Do not borrow money if you cannot pay it back.

H. Borrow money for any good reason. Good reasons are: to buy a house; to buy a car; to fix your house; to go into business.

*valuables — things that are important to a person, such as a passport or jewelry
*will — legal paper stating where your money, property and valuables go after your death
*maximum — the highest

POST OFFICE AND TELEPHONE

Post Office and Telephone

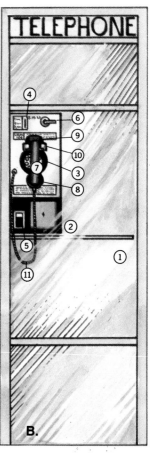

A. Post Office
1. postal clerk
2. scale
3. wrapping/brown paper
4. string
5. postman/mailman
6. mail bag
7. mail slot
8. package
9. mailing label
10. post office box

B. Telephone
1. phone booth
2. telephone
3. dial
4. coin slot
5. coin return
6. coin release
7. receiver
8. mouthpiece
9. earpiece
10. hook
11. cord

PRACTICE WITH PICTURES

1. stamp

2. envelope

3. address

4. return address

5. post card

6. Special Delivery

7. Air Mail

8. cellophane tape

9. return receipt

10. money order

11. mail box

12. mail truck

13. *Yellow Pages/ White Pages*

14. desk phone

15. push-button phone

16. dial

CONVERSATION 1: Mailing a Package

1.

A. I'd like to send this
   package to California.
B. How do you want to send it?

2.

A. Special Delivery.
B. Okay, I'll weigh it.

3.

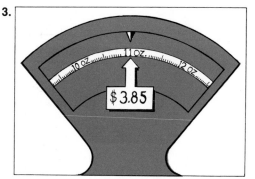

B. It weighs 11 ounces. That'll
   be $3.85 for Special Delivery.
A. That's expensive.

4.

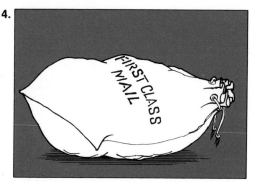

B. You can send it First Class for
   $2.25.
A. How long does it take?

5.

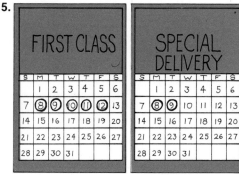

B. First Class takes five days.
   Special Delivery takes two days.
A. Send it First Class, please.

6.

A. I'd also like a book of
   stamps.
B. That'll be $6.50 total.

CONVERSATION 2: Asking for Information

1.

A. Operator, how do I get information in Oregon?
B. Dial Area Code 503, then dial 555-1212.

2.

C. Information, what city, please?
A. Portland.

3.

A. I'd like the number for Sam Pong.
C. How do you spell the last name?

4.

A. P as in plum, O as in orange, N as in nut, and G as in grapes.

5.

C. What's the address?
A. 19 Oak Lane.

6.

C. The number is 631-4582
A. Thanks very much.

CONVERSATION PLUS

Use the words in parentheses in each sentence below to make new sentences.

1. I'd like to send this **package** to California. (*post card, letter, money order*)
2. That's **expensive**. (*reasonable, cheap, high, too much, too little*)
3. Send it **First Class**, please. (*Second Class, Third Class, Fourth Class, Special Delivery, Express Mail*)
4. I'd also like **a book of** stamps. (*a few, a roll of, a sheet of*)
5. How do I get Information in **Oregon**? (*California, Arizona, Texas, New York*)
6. What **city** please? (*county, state, town*)
7. How do you spell the **last** name? (*first, middle*)
8. Thanks **very much**. (*so much, a lot*)

WHAT'S RIGHT?

Make the *appropriate* choice. Choose a, b, or c for each number below.

1. How do you want to send it?
   - ☐ a. That's expensive.
   - ☐ b. I'll weigh it.
   - ☐ c. Special Delivery.

2. ☐ a. It weighs 11 ounces.   That's expensive.
   - ☐ b. First Class takes five days.
   - ☐ c. That'll be $3.85 for Special Delivery.

3. ☐ a. How long does it take?   First Class takes five days.
    ☐ b. What's the address?
    ☐ c. How do you spell the last name?

4. How do I get Information in Oregon?   ☐ a. Portland.
    ☐ b. 631-4582.
    ☐ c. Dial Area Code 503,
         then dial 555-1212.

5. Information, what city please?   ☐ a. Sam Pong.
    ☐ b. Portland.
    ☐ c. P, as in plum.

6. ☐ a. How do I get information in
       Oregon?   P as in plum, O as in
    ☐ b. What city please?   orange, N as in nut, and G
    ☐ c. How do you spell the last name?   as in grapes.

7. What's the address?   ☐ a. 305-555-1212.
    ☐ b. 19 Oak Lane.
    ☐ c. 631-4582.

YOUR TURN

Fill in each response blank with an *appropriate* question or answer.

1. A. I'd like to send this package to California.

   B. _____

2. A. That'll be $3.85 for Special Delivery.

   B. _____

3. A. How long does it take?

   B. _____

4. A. How do I get Information in Oregon?

   B. _____

5. A. Information, what city please?

   B. _____

6. A. How do you spell the last name?

   B. _____

7. A. What's the address?

   B. _____

ROLE PLAY

1. You want to mail a package to another state or country. You ask the clerk at the Post Office to help you and he does. Ask about the different ways to send a package and the different costs.

   You:_____

   Clerk:_____

   You:_____

   Clerk:_____

   You:_____

   Clerk:_____

2. You want to find a telephone number for a person in a different state. You call Information and the Operator helps you. Ask the Operator for the number. Give the name and address of the person you are calling.

   You:_____

   Operator: _____

   You:_____

   Operator: _____

   You:_____

   Operator: _____

WORD PLAY

Complete the sentences below with the *appropriate* word from the Word List. You can use some words in more than one sentence.

Sentences

a. I'd like to send this _____ to California.

b. You can send it _____.

c. Where's the _____?

d. I'd like a _____.

e. I need a _____.

Word List

1. money order	11. mail slot
2. First Class	12. mailing label
3. phone booth	13. mail box
4. Fourth Class	14. Special Delivery
5. post card	15. stamp
6. telephone	16. cellophane tape
7. coin slot	17. return receipt
8. package	18. dial
9. string	19. *Yellow Pages*
10. Air Mail	

READING 1: Sending a Package

When you send a package, wrap it carefully. You can use newspaper or small pieces of plastic to protect the contents* of your package from moving around. Put the contents in a cardboard box and wrap it with heavy brown wrapping paper. Tie it with string or twine*. Write the mailing address* on the lower right part of the package. Write the return address* on the upper left part of the package. You can use a special mailing label for the address. Take the package to the *Parcel Post* desk in the Post Office. They will weigh it and tell you how much it will cost to send it.

*contents — what is inside the package
*twine — heavy wrapping string
*mailing address — place where the package is going
*return address — place where the package comes from

Catching On

Answer the following questions.

1. What can you use to protect the contents of the package?

2. What kind of box should you use?

3. What kind of paper would you wrap the box with?

4. What do you use string for?

5. Where do you write the mailing address?

6. Where do you write the return address?

7. Where do you take the package to mail it?

READING 2: Making a Call

Using a Pay Phone for Local Calls

You must use United States coins when using a pay phone. You can use nickels, dimes, or quarters. Listen for the dial tone first. Then put the coins in the slot and dial the number.

Making Long Distance Calls

You can make long distance calls from a pay phone or private phone. You can dial direct for long distance calls in the United States and many foreign countries.

There are many ways to pay for a phone call. You can reverse the charges. This means that the person you call will pay for the call. You can also charge the call to your home phone from any other phone. You can make a person-to-person call. This means you do not pay until you speak to the person that you are calling. If you need help with any of these special calls, dial Operator.

Just the Facts

Tell whether the following statements are true or false.

1. You must use United States coins when using a pay phone.
2. You can only use quarters in a pay phone.
3. First put the coins in and then listen for the dial tone.
4. You can only make long distance calls from a private phone.
5. You can dial direct for long distance calls in the United States and many foreign countries.
6. When you reverse charges the person you call will pay for the phone call.
7. You can't charge a call to your home phone from another phone.
8. A person-to-person call means that you don't pay until you speak to the person you are calling.

What Do You Think?

Answer the following questions.

1. Do you send many packages? Where do you send them?
2. What is the most difficult thing about mailing a package?

3. Do you like to talk on the phone? Tell why or why not.

4. Are long distance phone calls expensive in your country?

5. How do you use a pay phone in your country?

TALK IT OVER

Look at the map below. It shows the different time zones for the United States.

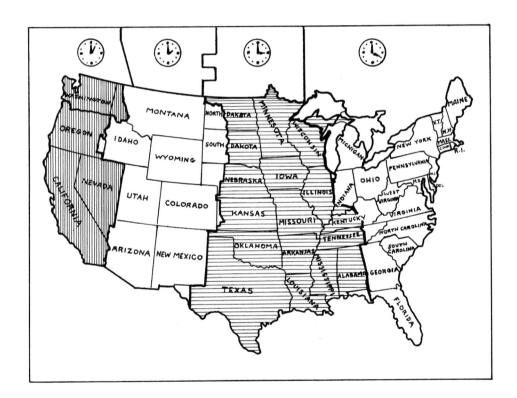

Work with other students in groups. Each person in the group lists the following information on the chart below: the states they are calling from; the time they are calling; the states they reach; and the time they reach the other states.

One person from each group reports the group's information to the class.

If you call from <u>Massachusetts</u> **at** <u>4:00 P.M.</u> **you reach** <u>Wyoming</u> **at** <u>2:00 P.M.</u>
     <u>California</u>   <u>8:30 A.M.</u>   <u>New York</u> <u>11:30 A.M.</u>

     ———   ———   ——— ———

     ———   ———   ——— ———

     ———   ———   ——— ———

     ———   ———   ——— ———

DO IT

There is an index at the back of the *Yellow Pages*. This index lists different categories* of businesses. *Example*: Restaurants and Hotels. A page number is listed next to the category.

Example: Restaurants 849
      Hotels   643

This means that the main address and phone number of many different restaurants are listed starting on page 849. The same information for hotels starts on page 643. Sometimes businesses include ads on these pages.

Choose any three categories you like. List the name, address, and phone number of one business in each category. Look at the ad for that business and list two features* from the ad.

*category — group or type
*features — something special about the company

	Category	Name of Business	Address	Phone Number	Feature 1	Feature 2
Example:	Auto Repair	Alpha Auto Repair	305 E. 12th Street	806-1274	Foreign car specialist	Free towing
1.	_____	_____	_____	_____	_____	_____
2.	_____	_____	_____	_____	_____	_____
3.	_____	_____	_____	_____	_____	_____

FOR YOUR INFORMATION

A. Postal Information:

1. If you want a letter or package to be delivered quickly, send it Express Mail or Special Delivery.

2. If you send something valuable, you can insure it. This means that if it is lost you will get money back.

3. You can register a letter or package. This means that the person who gets the package must sign for it. You will get a receipt if you ask for it.

4. If the Post Office loses your mail, fill out a *Consumer Service Card*. Get this card at the Post Office. The Post Office will try to find your letter or package.

B. Telephone:

1. It is cheaper to call long distance at night after 6 P.M. or on weekends.

2. There is a charge when you ask the Operator for information. Use the telephone book when possible.

3. If you get a wrong number, call the Operator. The Operator will give you credit for the call.

TRANSPORTATION

Transportation

1. bus
2. bus stop
3. passenger
4. taxi
5. driver
6. car
7. motorcycle
8. bicycle
9. street
10. sidewalk
11. crosswalk
12. intersection
13. traffic light
14. airplane
15. subway
16. station
17. platform

PRACTICE WITH PICTURES

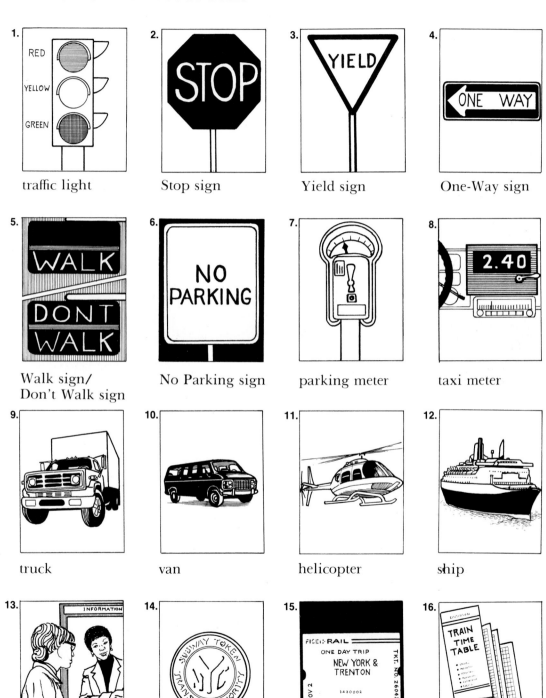

1. traffic light
2. Stop sign
3. Yield sign
4. One-Way sign
5. Walk sign/ Don't Walk sign
6. No Parking sign
7. parking meter
8. taxi meter
9. truck
10. van
11. helicopter
12. ship
13. information booth
14. token
15. ticket
16. time table

CONVERSATION 1: Going by Bus

1.

A. Does this bus go to Kraft Street?
B. No, take the number two bus.

2.

A. I want to go to Kraft Street.
C. Transfer to the number four bus at Green Street.

3.

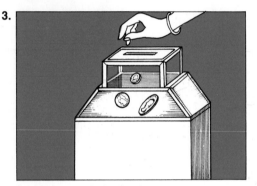

A. How much is the fare?
C. Eighty cents, exact change.

4.

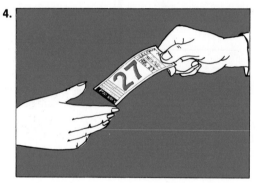

A. May I have a transfer, please?
C. Here it is.

5.

A. Please tell me when we get to Green Street.
C. It's the next street.

6.

C. Green Street.
A. Getting off, please.

CONVERSATION 2: Asking Directions

1.

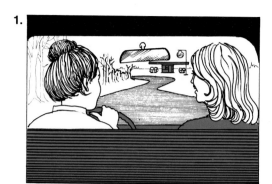

A. I think we're lost.
B. Yes, this doesn't look right.

2.

B. Let's ask directions.
A. Okay, I'll ask at the next gas station.

3.

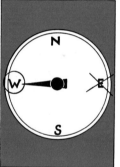

A. How do we get to Lodi?
C. You're going east, you should be going west.

4.

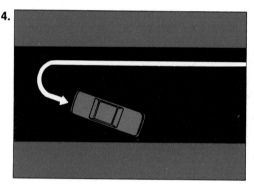

C. Make a U-turn and go straight for six blocks.
A. Then what do I do?

5.

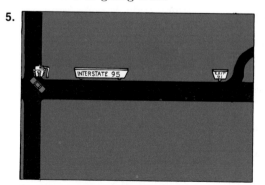

C. Turn right at the light. That's Interstate 95. Take Interstate 95 for two miles and get off at Exit 41.

6.

A. Thanks very much.
C. You can't miss it.
B. I hope not.

CONVERSATION PLUS

Use the words in parentheses in each sentence below to make new sentences.

1. I want to go to **Kraft Street.** (*the bus stop, the airport, the train station, the taxi stand*)
2. May I have a **transfer**, please? (*ticket, token, time table*)
3. I think **we're** lost. (*they're, you're, she's, he's, John's, I'm*)
4. You're going **east**. (*south, west, north*)
5. Make a **U-turn**. (*right turn, left turn, full stop*)
6. Go straight for six **blocks**. (*miles, lights, streets, stop signs*)
7. Get off at **Exit 41**. (*Green Street, the corner, Lodi, the station*)

WHAT'S RIGHT?

Make the *appropriate* choice. Choose a, b, or c for each number below.

1. Does this bus go to Kraft Street?

☐ a. Eighty cents, exact change.

☐ b. No, take the number two bus.

☐ c. Here it is.

2. I want to go to Kraft Street.

☐ a. No, take the number two bus.

☐ b. Green Street.

☐ c. Transfer to the number four bus at Green Street.

3. ☐ a. May I have a transfer please?

☐ b. How much is the fare?

☐ c. How do we get to Lodi?

Eighty cents, exact change.

4. ☐ a. How much is the fare?

☐ b. Does this bus go to Kraft Street?

☐ c. May I have a transfer please?

Here it is.

5. Please tell me when we get to Green Street.

☐ a. It's the next street.

☐ b. Transfer to the number four bus at Green Street.

☐ c. Take the number two bus.

6. Make a U-turn and go straight for six blocks.

☐ a. Yes, this doesn't look right.

☐ b. Then what do I do?

☐ c. Let's ask directions.

7. You can't miss it.

☐ a. Turn right at the light.

☐ b. I hope not.

☐ c. Let's ask directions.

YOUR TURN

Fill in each blank with an *appropriate* question or answer.

1. A. Does this bus go to Kraft Street?
   B. _____

2. A. _____
   B. Eighty cents, exact change.

3. A. _____
   B. Here it is.

4. A. Please tell me when we get to Green Street.
   B. _____

5. A. _____
   B. Yes, this doesn't look right.

6. A. _____
   B. Okay, I'll ask at the next gas station.

7. A. How do we get to Lodi?
   B. _____

8. A. _____
   B. Then what do I do?

ROLE PLAY

1. You want to go to Main Street by bus. You ask the bus driver for help and he helps you.

   You:_____

   Bus driver: _____

   You:_____

   Bus driver: _____

   You:_____

   Bus driver: _____

2. You are driving. You try to find Ludlow Street, but you are lost. You ask someone for directions and he or she helps you.

   You:_____

   Other person:_____

   You:_____

   Other person:_____

   You:_____

   Other person:_____

WORD PLAY

Complete the sentences below with the *appropriate* word from the Word List. You can use some words in more than one sentence.

Sentences

a. How do we get to the _____?

b. May I have a _____?

c. She wants a _____.

d. I want a _____.

e. Where's the _____?

Word List

1. station
2. token
3. airplane
4. ticket
5. bicycle
6. parking meter
7. traffic light
8. subway
9. motorcycle
10. Stop sign
11. transfer
12. bus stop
13. truck
14. van
15. time table

READING 1: Getting a Driver's License

The Motor Vehicles Bureau in every city gives information about driver's licenses and learner's permits. The number is listed in the *White Pages* of the telephone book.

If you don't know how to drive, you must apply for a learner's permit. If you have a learner's permit, a licensed driver must be in the car when you are driving. When you have learned how to drive, you must pass a road test, a written test, and an eye test to get your license. The road test shows that you can drive a car. The written test shows that you know the law. The eye test shows that you can read the signs. If you wear glasses, you can use them for the eye test.

You can go to a driving school to learn how to drive. The school has experienced teachers and they have special cars you can use for learning. These schools are listed in the *Yellow Pages* of the telephone book under "Driving Schools."

If you have a license from another country, call the Motor Vehicles Bureau to find out which tests you must take.

Catching On

Answer the following questions.

1. Where do you get information about driver's licenses and learner's permits?
2. What are the three tests you must pass to get a driver's license?
3. What does the road test show?
4. What does the written test show?
5. What does the eye test show?
6. Can you wear glasses when you take the eye test?
7. Where are driving schools listed?
8. If you have a driver's license from another country, what should you do?

READING 2: Traffic Signs

It is important to understand traffic signs. There are signs for drivers and signs for pedestrians*.

Some of the signs for drivers are the following:

1. *Traffic Light:* You must stop the car when the light is red. You may go when the light is green. The yellow light tells you that the light is going to change from green to red. You should begin to stop when you see the yellow light.
2. *Stop sign:* This means that you must stop the car before going ahead.
3. *No Parking sign:* When you see this sign, do not leave your car.
4. *One Way sign:* This means that cars can only go in one direction on that street.

Signs for pedestrians are the following:

1. *Walk sign:* This means you may cross the street in the crosswalk.
2. *Don't Walk sign:* This means that you must wait to cross the street. If the *Don't Walk* sign begins flashing when you are in the middle of the street, you should walk quickly to the other side.

*pedestrians — people who are walking

Just the Facts

Tell whether the following statements are true or false.

1. It's important to understand traffic signs.
2. There are only signs for pedestrians.
3. A Stop sign means that you should go very slowly.
4. A red light means that you must stop.
5. A green light means that you may go.
6. A yellow light means that you may cross the street.
7. A Don't Walk sign means that you must wait to cross the street.

What Do You Think?

Answer the following questions.

1. Would you like to drive a car? Tell why or why not.
2. Would you go to a driving school to learn how to drive? Tell why or why not.
3. How do people get a driver's license in your country?
4. Should there be a different road test in each country? Tell why or why not.

TALK IT OVER

Talk with other students in groups. Each group studies the map below. One person from each group tells the class how to get from *Start* to any *two* of the following places (the list of words on page 143 may help you):

1. Bus Stop
2. Airport
3. Subway

4. School
5. Restaurant
6. Post Office

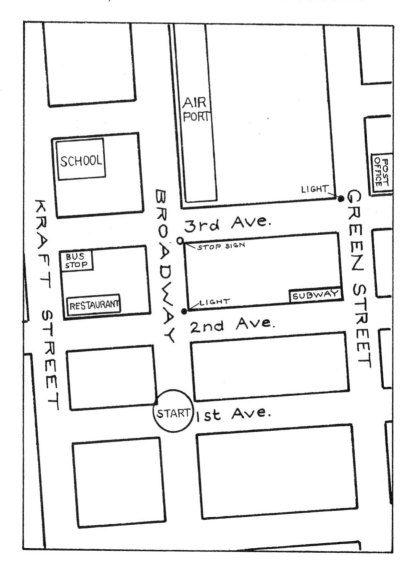

DO IT

Pretend that you are having a party at your house. You invite your classmates. On the invitation draw a map showing directions from the school to your house. Write out the directions, in words, from the school to your house. The following list may help you.

1. turn right	9. east
2. turn left	10. west
3. go to the _____.	11. bus
4. corner	12. train
5. go straight	13. taxi
6. take exit _____.	14. by car
7. north	15. walk
8. south	

FOR YOUR INFORMATION

A. Asking directions:

1. Ask a policeman.
2. Call the police station.
3. Ask at a gas station. You can also get a map at a gas station.
4. Call the transit system in your city for directions for trains or buses.

B. Getting help:

1. Call the Traveler's Aid Society if you are sick or need money while traveling.
2. Call your Embassy or delegation if you are from another country.

C. Using Traveler's Checks:

1. Many travelers carry traveler's checks instead of cash.
2. Keep a separate list of the numbers on your traveler's checks.
3. If you lose a traveler's check, call the company or bank where you got the checks. Tell them the number on your traveler's check, and the company or bank will replace the lost check.

D. Traffic violations:

1. Speed limits are on signs.
2. Don't go faster than the speed limit. You can lose your license for speeding.

SHOPPING FOR FOOD

Shopping for Food

1. shopper
2. checker/cashier
3. cash register
4. aisle
5. shopping cart
6. frozen food
7. ice cream
8. T.V. dinners
9. dairy
10. meat
11. fish
12. vegetables
13. tomato
14. green beans
15. cucumber
16. fruit
17. grapes
18. cherry
19. watermelon
20. cereal
21. beverages
22. crackers
23. toilet articles
24. canned goods
25. soap powder

PRACTICE WITH PICTURES

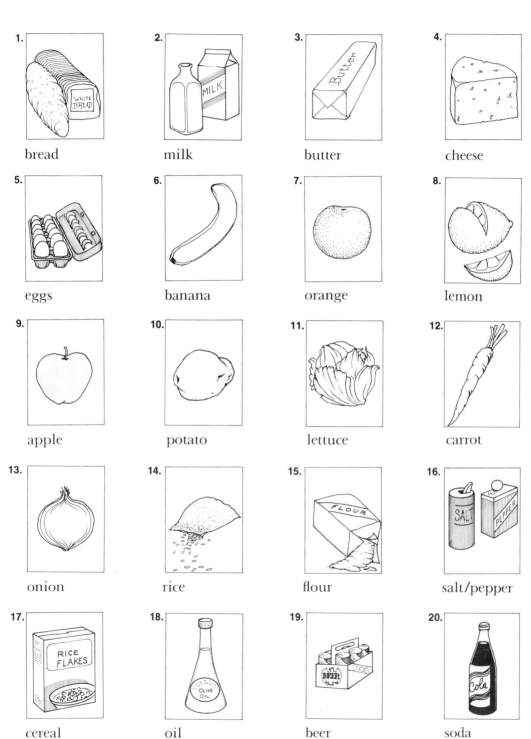

1. bread
2. milk
3. butter
4. cheese
5. eggs
6. banana
7. orange
8. lemon
9. apple
10. potato
11. lettuce
12. carrot
13. onion
14. rice
15. flour
16. salt/pepper
17. cereal
18. oil
19. beer
20. soda

CONVERSATION 1A: Shopping for Food

1.

A. Do you have the shopping list?
B. Yes, it's in my pocket.

2.

B. I'll get a cart.
A. Get two carts. We can shop faster.

3.

B. Here's half the shopping list.
A. Fine.

4.

B. How much is the soda?
C. It's $1.25 a bottle.

5.

B. Do you have any sugar?
D. Yes, it's in aisle four on the bottom shelf.

6.

A. I want a pound of apples. How much are they?
D. They're 89¢ a pound.

CONVERSATION 1B: Shopping for Food

1.

B. I want a pound of rice. How much is it?
C. It's $1.25 a pound.

2.

A. How much are the rolls?
E. They're 20¢ each.
A. I'll take four.

3.

A. We need eggs.
B. I have a dozen.

4.

B. Do you want a bag of potato chips?
A. No, we don't need them.

5.

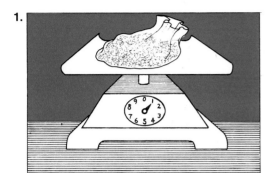

B. You get in line and I'll get the check approved.
A. Okay, I'll meet you there.

6.

F. That'll be $60.82.
A. The price of food gets higher all the time.

CONVERSATION PLUS

Use the words in parentheses in each sentence below to make new sentences.

1. How much is the **soda**? (*coffee, tea, beer*)
2. How much are the **rolls**? (*potatoes, carrots, eggs, onions*)
3. Do you have any **sugar**? (*rice, flour, salt, pepper*)
4. I want a pound of **apples**. (*cherries, oranges, lemons, bananas*)
5. I want a pound of **rice**. (*butter, cheese, coffee*)
6. It's $1.25 **a bottle**. (*a pound, a dozen, a can, a box, a six-pack, each*)
7. **I'll** take four. (*She'll, He'll, You'll, They'll, We'll*)
8. The price of food gets **higher** all the time. (*lower, cheaper*)

WHAT'S RIGHT?

Make the *appropriate* choice. Choose a, b, or c for each number below.

1. Here's half the shopping list.

☐ a. Fine.
☐ b. That's okay.
☐ c. I'll take four.

2. How much is the soda?

☐ a. It's $1.25 a pound.
☐ b. It's $1.25 a bottle.
☐ c. It's $1.25 a bag.

3. How much are they?

☐ a. It's 89¢ a bottle.

☐ b. It's 89¢ a pound.

☐ c. They're 89¢ a pound.

4. How much is it?

☐ a. They're $1.25 a pound.

☐ b. It's $1.25 a pound.

☐ c. They're $1.25 each.

5. ☐ a. We need rice.   I have a dozen.

  ☐ b. No, we don't need them.

  ☐ c. We need eggs.

6. ☐ a. Do you want a bag of potato chips?   No, we don't need them.

  ☐ b. I have a dozen.

  ☐ c. I want a pound of flour.

YOUR TURN

Fill in each blank with an *appropriate* question or answer.

1. A. Do you have the shopping list?
   B. _____

2. A. _____
   B. It's $1.25 a bottle.

3. A. Do you have any sugar?
   B. _____

4. A. I want a pound of apples. How much are they?
   B. _____

5. A. I want a pound of rice.
   B. _____

6. A. _____
   B. They're 20¢ each.

7. A. We need eggs.
   B. _____

8. A. _____
   B. No, we don't need them.

ROLE PLAY

1. You are in a supermarket. You ask the clerk the price of soda, eggs, potatoes, rice, rolls, and apples. The clerk tells you.

You:_____

Clerk:_____

You:_____

Clerk:_____

You:_____

Clerk:_____

You:_____

Clerk:_____

You:_____

Clerk:_____

You:_____

Clerk:_____

WORD PLAY

Complete the sentences below with the *appropriate* word from the Word List. You can use some words in more than one sentence.

Sentences

a. I want a pound of _____.

b. I want a bottle of _____.

c. I want a package of _____.

d. I want a dozen _____.

e. I want a can of _____.

f. I want a six-pack of _____.

g. I want a bag of _____.

pound

bottle

package   dozen   can   six-pack   bag

Word List

1. coffee	6. eggs	11. flour	16. bananas
2. butter	7. lemons	12. rice	17. potatoes
3. beer	8. apples	13. cereal	18. sugar
4. soda	9. oranges	14. salt	19. onions
5. potato chips	10. cheese	15. rolls	20. oil

READING 1: Unit Pricing

Many supermarkets use unit pricing to help people save money. The following examples show how unit pricing works.

Item	Size	Price of Item	Unit Price Per Pound
Soap Powder	1 pound	$1.00	$1.00
	3 pounds	$2.75	$0.92*
	5 pounds	$4.00	$0.80
Rice	1 pound	$0.69	$0.69
	3 pounds	$1.75	$0.58
	5 pounds	$2.50	$0.50

Usually if you buy the larger amount you save money, but if you buy too much it may spoil and you will lose money.

Unit pricing is for food in a can, package, or a bottle. The unit price is marked on the shelf above or below the item.

*$0.92=92¢

Catching On

Answer the following questions.

1. Who uses unit pricing?
2. How much does 3 pounds of soap powder cost?
3. How much does 5 pounds of soap powder cost?
4. How much does 3 pounds of soap powder cost per pound?
5. How much does 5 pounds of soap powder cost per pound?
6. How much do you save per pound if you buy 5 pounds of soap powder and not 3 pounds?
7. Do you always save money if you buy the larger amount?
8. Where is the unit price marked?

READING 2: Saving Money in the Supermarket

There are many ways to save money in the supermarket. You can use coupons. You can read the ads for food in the newspapers. You can compare prices of different brands*. You can look for stores that are having a sale*.

You can find coupons in the newspaper, in the mail, and at the supermarket. Coupons save you money on certain items. The name of the item and the amount you save is on the coupon. Coupons look like this:

Coupons come in different amounts but are usually from 10¢ to $1.00. There is also a date on the coupon. You cannot use the coupon after that date. Take the coupon with you to the store.

*brand — name of the company that makes an item
*sale — lower prices on certain items for a short time

Just the Facts

Tell whether the following statements are true or false.

1. There are many ways to save money in the supermarket.
2. All brands cost the same.
3. All coupons are for 10¢.
4. Some stores have sales.
5. Take the coupon with you to the store.
6. You can use the same coupon for any item.

Catching On

Answer the following questions.

1. Name two ways to save money in the supermarket.
2. Where do you find ads for food?
3. Name two places where you can find coupons.
4. Name two things that are on the coupon.
5. Where should you take the coupon?

What Do You Think?

Answer the following questions.

1. Do you read the unit price signs in the supermarket? Tell why or why not.
2. Do you like to buy small or large sizes of food? Tell why.
3. Do you like to shop in supermarkets or in small stores? Tell why.
4. Do you have coupons in your country?
5. Do you use coupons? Tell why or why not.

TALK IT OVER

Talk with other students in groups. Each group goes to a different supermarket or food store. Each group gets the price of the items on the list below. One person from each group reads their prices and the class discusses the differences.

Item	Price
1. one pound of apples	1. _____
2. one pound of oranges	2. _____
3. one pound of carrots	3. _____
4. one pound of tomatoes	4. _____
5. five pounds of rice	5. _____
6. five pounds of potatoes	6. _____
7. five pounds of coffee	7. _____
8. five pounds of flour	8. _____
9. six-pack of soda	9. _____
10. one dozen large eggs	10. _____

DO IT

Make a shopping list of food that you would buy for one week. List the items you generally buy. List the amount you buy of each item under the *appropriate* column, depending on whether you shop for one person (yourself), two people, or a family of four or more. Then exchange lists with your classmates. Discuss the lists.

Item	Amount for One Person	Amount for Two People	Amount for a Family of Four or More
1. apples	3	1 pound	5 pounds
2.			
3.			
4.			
5.			
6.			
7.			
8.			
9.			
10.			
11.			
12.			
13.			
14.			
15.			

FOR YOUR INFORMATION

A. Be careful about the following things:

   1. A can that does not look right. The food in that can can make you sick.

   2. Packages that are open.

   3. Cracked eggs.

B. Food Stamps:

   If you don't have enough money to buy food, you can apply for food stamps. For more information, call the United States Department of Agriculture in your city. The telephone number is listed in the *White Pages* of your telephone book.

C. No Frills:

   Many supermarkets have a shelf of items called "No Frills." These are foods in cans and packages. The cans and packages come in plain white paper with black letters. They do not use brand names. These items are cheaper than other items in the store.

SHOPPING FOR CLOTHES

Shopping for Clothes

1. salesman	13. tie
2. tailor	14. socks
3. suit	15. shoes
4. vest	16. saleswoman
5. sport jacket	17. blouse
6. lapel	18. skirt
7. sleeve	19. dress
8. button	20. pantsuit
9. pocket	21. hem
10. pants/slacks	22. belt
11. cuff	23. buckle
12. shirt	24. jeans

PRACTICE WITH PICTURES

1. raincoat

2. shorts

3. turtleneck

4. sweater

5. coat

6. pajamas

7. bathrobe

8. slipper

9. bra

10. panties

11. pantyhose

12. slip

13. short

14. long

15. big

16. small

CONVERSATION 1: Buying a Gift

A. I'd like to buy a gift for
   my husband.
B. How about a tie?

B. What color does he like?
A. His favorite color is brown.

B. This is a beautiful brown
   tie.
A. Do you have a dark brown one?
B. Yes, but it's striped.

A. That one is very nice. How
   much is it?
B. $12.50.

A. I'll take it.
B. Is this cash or charge?
A. I'll pay cash.

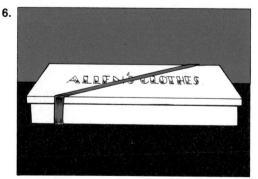

B. I'll gift wrap it.
A. I hope he likes it.
B. I'm sure he will.

CONVERSATION 2: Buying a Dress

1.

A. Can I help you?
B. Yes, I'm looking for a dress.

2.

A. What kind?
B. An everyday dress.

3.

A. What size do you wear?
B. Size 12.

4.

A. I have a red print dress and
   a yellow plaid.
B. I like the red print.

5.

B. Can I try it on?
A. Yes, the dressing room is
   over there.

6.

B. I'm sorry, I don't like it.
A. That's okay. Come back again.

CONVERSATION PLUS

Use the words in parentheses in each sentence below to make new sentences.

1. I'd like to buy a gift for my **husband**. (*son, daughter, wife*)
2. His favorite color is **brown**. (*blue, tan, grey, yellow*)
3. This is a **beautiful** brown tie. (*handsome, lovely, good-looking, nice*)
4. It's **striped**. (*checked,   plaid,   a print,   solid*)

5. I'll **take** it. (*leave, charge, send, buy, return*)
6. I hope he **likes** it. (*wants, needs, wears*)
7. I'm looking for a **dress**. (*skirt, blouse, coat, sweater*)
8. The dressing room is **over there**. (*over here, here, there, upstairs, downstairs*)

WHAT'S RIGHT?

Make the *appropriate* choice. Choose a, b, or c for each number below.

1. I'd like to buy a gift for my husband. ☐ a. How about a tie?
   ☐ b. It's $12.50.
   ☐ c. That's okay.

2. What color does he like?

☐ a. His favorite color is brown.

☐ b. I have a red print dress and a yellow plaid.

☐ c. But it's striped.

3. ☐ a. What color does he like?

☐ b. What size do you wear?

☐ c. How much is it?

It's $12.50.

4. ☐ a. Can I help you?

☐ b. Is this cash or charge?

☐ c. What kind?

I'll pay cash.

5. ☐ a. Do you have a dark brown one?

☐ b. Can I help you?

☐ c. Can I try it on?

Yes, I'm looking for a dress.

6. I hope he likes it.

☐ a. I'll pay cash.

☐ b. I'll gift wrap it.

☐ c. I'm sure he will.

7. I'm sorry, I don't like it.

☐ a. That's okay. Come back again.

☐ b. Yes, but it's striped.

☐ c. I'll gift wrap it.

YOUR TURN

Fill in each blank with an *appropriate* question or answer.

1. A. I'd like to buy a gift for my husband.
   B. _____

2. A. What color does he like?
   B. _____

3. A. _____
   B. It's $12.50.

4. A. _____
   B. I'll pay cash.

5. A. I hope he likes it.
   B. _____

6. A. Can I help you?
   B. _____

7. A. What size do you wear?
   B. _____

8. A. _____
   B. That's okay. Come back again.

ROLE PLAY

1. You want to buy a tie. You tell the salesperson the color you want and the salesperson helps you.

   You:_____

   Salesperson: _____

   You:_____

   Salesperson: _____

   You:_____

   Salesperson: _____

2. You want to buy a woman's dress. You tell the salesperson the size and color you want and the salesperson helps you.

   You:_____

   Salesperson: _____

   You:_____

   Salesperson: _____

   You:_____

   Salesperson: _____

WORD PLAY

Choose the word that is *inappropriate* in each group.

1. raincoat, sweater, coat, pajamas
2. bathrobe, pajamas, slipper, turtleneck
3. skirt, sport jacket, dress, blouse
4. bra, panties, pantyhose, dress
5. belt, buckle, button, pants
6. salesman, tailor, hem, saleswoman
7. shorts, long, big, small, short

READING 1: Sizes for Men

Sizes in the United States are different from those in most other countries. The drawings below show clothes sizes for small, medium, and large men.

	Figure A	Figure B	Figure C
Suit and Jacket	32 →36	37 →42	44 →50
Shirt: Collar	12 →13	14 →16	17 →20
Sleeve	28 →30	30 →34	35 →38
Shorts } Slacks	24→ 30	31→ 36	38 →44
Sweater } Sport Shirt	Small	Medium	Large
Shoes: Length	6 →8	9 →11	12 →14
Width	A,B,C,D,E	A,B,C,D,E	A,B,C,D,E

When you buy a suit or jacket, give the size number and tell whether you want a short, regular, or long jacket. *For example*: **Figure A** in the drawing might buy a "36 short." When you buy a shirt, give the collar size first and then the sleeve size. *For example*: **Figure B** might buy a "14½-30." When you buy shorts or slacks give the waist* size. *For example*: **Figure C** might buy a "Size 40." When you buy shoes, give the length* and width*. The number tells the length. The letter tells the width. *For example*: **Figure B** might buy a "9 D."

If you have any questions about your size, ask the salesperson.

*waist — where your belt goes
*length — long
*width — wide

Just the Facts

Tell whether the following statements are true or false.

1. Sizes in the U.S. are the same as in other countries.
2. Figure A might buy a "36 Short" suit.
3. Figure C might buy a "40 Regular" suit.
4. Figure B might buy a "14½-30" shirt.
5. Figure C might buy a "15½-33" shirt.
6. Figure C might buy a "Size 40" shorts.
7. Figure B might buy a "9 D" shoe.
8. Figure A might buy a "10 C" shoe.

READING 2: Sizes for Women

Sizes for women's clothes are also different in the U.S. The drawings below show clothes sizes for small, medium, and large women.

Figure D **Figure E** **Figure F**

	Figure D	Figure E	Figure F
Dress			
Skirt			
Blouse			
	5 7 9	11 13	15 Junior
	6 8 10	12 14	16 18 Misses
Slacks			
Jacket			
Coat			
Sweater	Small	Medium	Large
Shoes: Length	5-6	7-8	9-10
Width	A,B,C,D,E	A,B,C,D,E	A,B,C,D,E

Sizes 6 to 18 are "Misses Sizes." These are usually for older women. Sizes 5 to 15 are "Junior Sizes." These are usually for younger women. *For example*: An 18-year-old medium-sized woman might buy a "Size 11" dress. A small woman over 35 might buy a "Size 8" dress. When you buy shoes give the length and width. *For example*: **Figure E** might buy a size "7 B" shoe and **Figure D** might buy a "5 A." Sweaters usually come in small, medium, or large.

If you have any questions about your size, ask the salesperson.

Just the Facts

Tell whether the following statements are true or false.

1. Figure E might buy a "Size 14" skirt.
2. Figure D might buy a "Size 8" slacks.
3. Figure F might buy a "Size 16" coat.
4. "Size 15" is a Misses size.
5. "Size 16" is a Misses size.
6. A small woman over 35 might buy a "Size 8" dress.
7. Figure D might buy a "5 A" shoe.
8. Figure F might buy a "7 D."

What Do You Think?

Answer the following questions.

1. Should sizes be the same throughout the world? Tell why or why not.
2. Where do you buy your clothes? Tell why.
3. What type of clothes do you like to wear? Tell why.
4. Are the clothes in your country different from those in the United States? Tell about them.

TALK IT OVER

Fill out the questionnaire below for three people in your class. Circle whether the person is a man or a woman. When you have the information, share it with the class.

Questionnaire on Clothing

Questions	1. Man/Woman	2. Man/Woman	3. Man/Woman
1. What is your favorite color?			
2. What gift would you buy for your mother?			
3. What gift would you buy for your father?			
4. What gift would you buy for your husband/wife/friend?			
5. What gift would you buy for yourself?			
6. Would you pay cash or charge?			

DO IT

There are two size cards below. Fill one out with your sizes. You can give it to your spouse* or friend so they can shop for you.

Ask your spouse or friend to fill out the other size card. You can use it to shop for them.

*spouse — husband or wife

SIZE CARD—MEN	
Item	**Size**
Suit	____ ____
Shirt	____ ____
Shorts	_____
Slacks	_____
Sweater/ Sport Shirt	_____
Shoes	____ ____

SIZE CARD—WOMEN	
Item	**Size**
Dress	_____
Skirt	_____
Blouse	_____
Sweater	_____
Coat	_____
Jacket	_____
Shoes	____ ____

FOR YOUR INFORMATION

A. Where To Buy Clothes:

1. Department stores sell many different things. They may sell furniture, toys, books, and clothes. The stores usually have many different types of clothes for men and women.
2. Clothing stores are smaller than department stores. There are clothing stores for men and clothing stores for women. They often sell one type of clothes.
3. Discount clothing stores sell clothes cheaper than other stores.
4. Some stores sell used clothes. They are sometimes called "Thrift Shops." These stores can be cheaper than discount stores.

B. Types of Clothes:

1. Some clothes are called "Wash and Wear." This means that you can wash them yourself.
2. Some clothes are called "Permanent Press." This means that they don't have to be pressed*.
3. Some clothes must be dry-cleaned. This means that you must take them to a dry-cleaning store.

C. Things To Be Careful About:

1. Always try on clothes before you buy them.
2. Look for holes or dirt before you buy the clothes.
3. Ask if you can exchange the clothes.
4. Ask if you can return the clothes and get your money back.
5. Keep all receipts and sales slips.

D. Complaints:

If you have a complaint, talk to the Manager. If the Manager can't help you, call the Office of Consumer Affairs. This number is listed in the *White Pages* of your telephone book.

*pressed — ironed

SHOPPING FOR FURNITURE

Shopping for Furniture

A. Bedroom
1. bed
2. mattress
3. (box) spring
4. headboard
5. night table
6. lamp
7. clock-radio
8. dresser
9. drawer
10. handle
11. dressing table
12. mirror
13. chest of drawers

B. Linens
1. blanket
2. quilt
3. sheet
4. pillow
5. pillow case
6. bedspread
7. tablecloth
8. napkin
9. towel

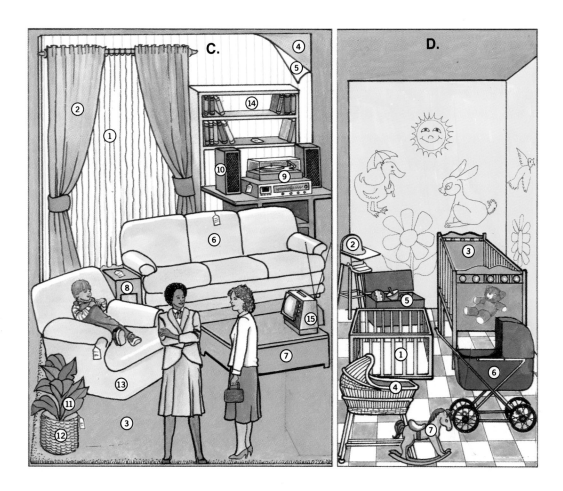

C. Living Room

1. curtain
2. drape
3. carpet
4. wall
5. wallpaper
6. couch/sofa
7. coffee table
8. end table
9. stereo/hi-fi
10. speaker
11. plant
12. basket
13. chair
14. bookcase
15. television

D. Baby's Room

1. playpen
2. highchair
3. crib
4. bassinet
5. toy chest/toy box
6. baby carriage
7. rocking horse

PRACTICE WITH PICTURES

1. slipcover

2. (Venetian) blind

3. (window) shade

4. coat rack

5. umbrella stand

6. picture

7. magazine rack

8. desk

9. rocking chair

10. lounge chair/ lounger

11. stool

12. footstool

13. piano

14. bench

15. wood

16. metal

CONVERSATION 1: Buying a Table

1.

A. Where are the tables?
B. Upstairs on the second floor.
   Take the escalator up.

2.

C. We're looking for a table.
D. What kind, sir?
C. A dining room table.

3.

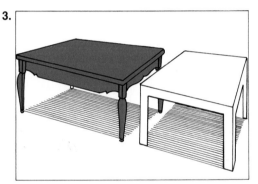

D. We have many tables. Would
   you like modern or traditional?
A. Modern.

4.

D. This one is made of oak.
A. I'd prefer walnut.

5.

D. Here's a lovely walnut table.
   It seats six people.
C. I like it.
A. Me too. Let's buy it.

6.

C. When can you deliver it?
D. In two weeks.

CONVERSATION 2: Buying a Bedroom Set

1.

A. Do you have any bedroom sets?
B. Yes, we do. What kind of bed do you want?

2.

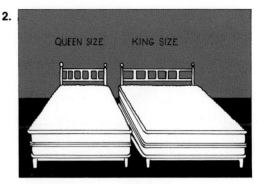

C. I'd like a queen-sized bed.
A. I'd like a king-sized, it's larger.

3.

C. Do you have a firm mattress?
B. This is the firmest we have.

4.

A. We also need a dresser and two night tables.
B. Do you like these?

5.

A. I like those better.
B. Is there anything else?
C. No, that's all, thanks.

6.

B. Do you want to charge it?
C. Yes, here's my credit card.

CONVERSATION PLUS

Use the words in parentheses in each sentence below to make new sentences.

1. Where are the **tables**? (*chairs, bookcases, lamps, mirrors*)
2. Upstairs on the **second** floor. (*third, fourth, fifth, sixth*)
3. This one is made of **oak**. (*walnut, pine, wood, metal, plastic*)
4. It seats **six** people. (*eight, ten, twelve*)
5. I'd like a **queen-sized** bed. (*king-sized, double, twin, single*)
6. It's **larger**. (*bigger, smaller, firmer, softer*)
7. This is the **firmest** we have. (*largest, biggest, smallest, softest*)
8. I like **those** better. (*these, this, that*)

WHAT'S RIGHT?

Make the *appropriate* choice. Choose a, b, or c for each number below.

1. Where are the tables?
   - ☐ a. Upstairs on the second floor.
   - ☐ b. It seats six people.
   - ☐ c. In two weeks.

2. Would you like modern or traditional?
   - ☐ a. This one is made of oak.
   - ☐ b. I'd prefer walnut.
   - ☐ c. Modern.

3. ☐ a. We're looking for a table.   Me too. Let's buy it.
    ☐ b. I like it.
    ☐ c. It seats six people.

4. ☐ a. Would you like modern or   In two weeks.
        traditional?
    ☐ b. Where are the tables?
    ☐ c. When can you deliver it?

5. Do you have any bedroom sets?   ☐ a. This is the firmest
                                    we have.
                               ☐ b. Yes, we do.
                               ☐ c. I'd like a king-sized.

6. Do you have a firm mattress?   ☐ a. This is the firmest
                                    we have.
                               ☐ b. It's larger.
                               ☐ c. I like those better.

7. Is there anything else?   ☐ a. This is the firmest
                                    we have.
                               ☐ b. No, that's all, thanks.
                               ☐ c. This one is made of oak.

8. Do you want to charge it?   ☐ a. In two weeks.
                                 ☐ b. I like it.
                               ☐ c. Yes, here's my credit card.

YOUR TURN

Fill in each blank with an *appropriate.* question or answer.

1. A. _____
   B. Upstairs on the second floor.

2. A. _____
   B. Modern.

3. A. _____
   B. Me too, let's buy it.

4. A. When can you deliver it?
   B. _____

5. A. What kind of bed do you want?
   B. _____

6. A. Do you have a firm mattress?
   B. _____

7. A. Is there anything else?
   B. _____

8. A. _____
   B. Yes, here's my credit card.

ROLE PLAY

1. You want to buy a table. You tell the salesperson what you want and the salesperson helps you.

    You: _____

    Salesperson: _____

    You: _____

    Salesperson: _____

    You: _____

    Salesperson: _____

2. You want to buy a bedroom set. You tell the salesperson what you want and the salesperson helps you.

    You: _____

    Salesperson: _____

    You: _____

    Salesperson: _____

    You: _____

    Salesperson: _____

WORD PLAY

Choose the word that is *inappropriate* in each group.

1. spring, mattress, bed, lamp
2. couch, dressing table, dresser, night table
3. clock-radio, television, stereo, headboard
4. blanket, pillow, handle, sheet
5. dresser, chest of drawers, dressing table, carpet
6. curtain, drape, chair, window shade
7. bassinet, coffee table, crib, playpen

READING: Buying on Credit

You can buy furniture and other things on credit. You can get a charge card from a store. This is a card for credit at one store. It means you have a charge account at that store. Most large stores have their own charge cards. Apply directly to the store for this card. You can also use a credit card. This is a card from a credit company or bank. *Visa, American Express,* and *MasterCard* are examples of major credit cards. You can use these credit cards at many different stores, restaurants, and hotels. There are application forms for major credit cards at banks, restaurants, and hotels.

There are two kinds of credit: monthly accounts and revolving accounts. Monthly accounts must be paid in-full* every month. You don't have to pay interest* in this type of account. In a revolving account, you pay a part of the total bill. You also pay interest on the unpaid balance. The interest can be as high as 20%. This means that you are paying much more than the cost of the furniture. Credit cards are useful, but they can also be expensive.

*in-full — completely
*interest — extra charge for using credit

Catching On

Answer the following questions.

1. Where do you get a charge card?
2. Name two major credit cards.
3. Where can you use major credit cards?
4. Where do you get application forms for major credit cards?
5. Name two kinds of credit.
6. What is interest?
7. How do you pay a monthly account?
8. How do you pay a revolving account?

What Do You Think?

Answer the following questions.

1. What is good about using credit cards?
2. What is bad about using credit cards?
3. Would you pay cash for furniture?
4. Do you have credit cards in your country? Tell how they work.
5. Would you use a credit card?

TALK IT OVER

Work with another student in pairs. First, **Student A** in each pair describes his living room furniture and tells how it is arranged. **Student B** draws the furniture that **Student A** is describing in *Room 1* on the next page. Then, **Student B** describes his living room furniture and **Student A** draws the furniture that **Student B** is describing in *Room 2* on the next page.

Room 1

North

West

East

South

Room 2

North

West

East

South

DO IT

Most people use credit cards to buy furniture. Fill out the sample credit card application below.

FIRST NATIONAL BANK - Card Services Department Application

1. TELL US ABOUT YOURSELF (Title Optional) ☐ Mr. ☐ Mrs. ☐ Miss ☐ Ms.

| Full Name (Please Print) | First | Middle | Last | | | Social Security Number | |

| Present Home Address | Number and Street | Apt. No. | City | State | Zip Code | | Years There |

| Area Code ( ) | Home Phone | ☐ Monthly Rent $_____ ☐ Own Mortgage $_____ | Date of Birth / / | No. of Dependents (include self) | List Automobiles Owned Year   Make |

| Previous Home Address | Number and Street | Apt. No. | City | State | Zip Code | Years There |

2. TELL US ABOUT YOUR INCOME

| Present Employer or Business | Name |

| Business Address | Number and Street | City | State | Zip Code | Years There |

| Area Code Business Phone ( ) | Position | Dept. Name/ No. | Employee/ Badge No. | Annual Income $ |

| Previous Employer or Business | | Position |

| Business Address | Number and Street | City | State | Zip Code | Years There |

3. TELL US ABOUT YOUR CREDIT REFERENCES (Please indicate if the name on the account is different than the one you have used on this application.)

| Savings Account | Bank Name and Address | Account Number |
| Checking Account | | |

Name and Address of nearest relative not living with you.   Relationship

Have you ever applied to this Bank for a Personal Loan or Credit Card? ☐ Yes ☐ No   If yes, list current _____ Account Numbers _____

4. OTHER INFORMATION

If your spouse* will use this account, please indicate name below, so we may report your account in both names.

Spouse's Name _____
Spouse Signs Here   X _____   Date _____
Applicant Signs Here   X _____   Date _____

---

*spouse – husband or wife

FOR YOUR INFORMATION

A. Care of Furniture:

1. To protect your furniture, use furniture polish.
2. For small burns on furniture, rub mayonnaise into the burn. After a few minutes, wipe it off with a soft cloth.
3. For small scratches, put Vaseline on the wood. Leave it on for twenty-four hours. Then rub it into the wood.
4. For grease and oil stains, pour salt on immediately.

For major problems, look under "Furniture Repair" in the *Yellow Pages* of your telephone book.

B. Credit Cards:

1. Keep a list of your credit card numbers.
2. If you lose a credit card, call the credit company immediately. Give them your credit card number and tell them that you lost your card and need a new one.
3. If there is a problem with your bill, write a letter to the company. Don't telephone the company. If you write to the company about the part of the bill that you think is wrong, you don't have to pay that part until you and the company agree about the bill.

SCHOOL AND
DAY CARE CENTERS

School and Day Care Centers

A. Pre-school/Kindergarten

1. teacher
2. child
3. smock
4. easel
5. brush
6. paint
7. scissors
8. construction paper
9. block
10. cookie
11. juice
12. cot
13. blanket
14. teddy bear

B. The Playground

1. seesaw/teeter-totter
2. shovel
3. pail/bucket
4. monkey bars/jungle gym
5. sandbox
6. swing
7. slide
8. trampoline

PRACTICE WITH PICTURES

1. crayon

2. clay

3. puzzle

4. pad of paper

5. mudpie

6. Magic Marker

7. pencil

8. pencil sharpener

9. ruler

10. glove/mitt

11. ball

12. bat

13. jump rope

14. doll

15. doll carriage

16. kite

CONVERSATION 1A: Choosing a Day Care Center

1.

A. I'd like to enroll my son.
B. How old is he?

2.

A. He's 3½. He's very shy.

3.

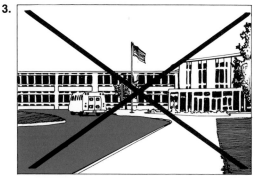

B. Has he been to school before?
A. No, he hasn't.

4.

B. Is he an only child?
A. No, he has an older sister
and brother.

5.

A. What do the children do here
all day?
B. In the morning we read stories,
paint, draw, and build blocks.

6.

A. Do you serve a hot lunch?
B. Yes, we do.

CONVERSATION 1B: Choosing a Day Care Center

7.

B. The children get meat or fish,
   a vegetable, fruit, and milk.
A. That sounds very good.

8.

B. After lunch they have rest
   hour.
A. What do they do after rest
   hour?

9.

B. They play in the playground.
A. How many children are in a group?
B. There are six in each group.

10.

A. Are all of your teachers licensed?
B. Yes, they all have state
   licenses.

11.

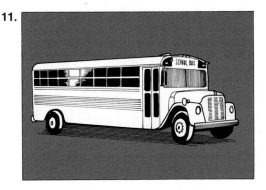

A. Do you have transportation?
B. Yes, we have free bus service.

12.

B. I think your son will be
   happy here.
A. So do I.

CONVERSATION PLUS

Use the words in parentheses in each sentence below to make new sentences.

1. How old is **he**? (*she, the child, your son, your daughter*)
2. He's very **shy**. (*active, quiet, happy, sad*)
3. What do the children do here **all day**? (*in the morning, in the afternoon, later, after rest hour*)
4. Do you serve **a hot lunch**? (*a snack, juice, cookies, breakfast*)
5. That sounds **very good**. (*excellent, wonderful, great, fine*)
6. How many children are in a **group**? (*class, section, room*)
7. Are **all** of your teachers licensed? (*some, any, many*)

WHAT'S RIGHT?

Make the *appropriate* choice. Choose a, b, or c for each number below.

1. How old is he?

☐ a. He's very shy.
☐ b. He's 3½.
☐ c. I'd like to enroll my son.

2. Has he been to school before?

☐ a. So do I.
☐ b. Yes, we do.
☐ c. No, he hasn't.

3. ☐ a. Is he an only child?   No, he has an older

   ☐ b. How old is he?   sister and brother.

   ☐ c. Do you have transportation?

4. ☐ a. What do the children do here all day?   Yes, we do.

   ☐ b. Has he been to school before?

   ☐ c. Do you serve a hot lunch?

5. How many children are in a group?   ☐ a. He's 3½.

                                        ☐ b. There are six in each
                                              group.

                                        ☐ c. No, he has an older
                                            sister and brother.

6. Are all of your teachers licensed?   ☐ a. No, he hasn't.

                                        ☐ b. Yes, we do.

                                        ☐ c. Yes, they all have
                                            state licenses.

7. Do you have transportation?   ☐ a. After lunch they
                                            have rest hour.

                                        ☐ b. Yes, we have free
                                            bus service.

                                        ☐ c. Yes, they all have
                                            state licenses.

8. I think your son will be happy here.   ☐ a. So do I.

                                        ☐ b. He's 3½.

                                      ☐ c. No, he hasn't.

YOUR TURN

Fill in each blank with an *appropriate* question or answer.

1. A. How old is he?
   B. _____

2. A. Has he been to school before?
   B. _____

3. A. _____
   B. No, he has an older sister and brother.

4. A. _____
   B. In the morning we read stories, paint, draw, and build blocks.

5. A. Do you serve a hot lunch?
   B. _____

6. A. _____
   B. There are six in each group.

7. A. Do you have transportation?
   B. _____

8. A. _____
   B. So do I.

ROLE PLAY

1. You speak to the director of the day care center. You ask her about the center and she tells you. You ask about food, teachers, transportation, equipment, and activities. She answers your questions.

You: _____

Director: _____

You: _____

Director: _____

You: _____

Director: _____

You: _____

Director: _____

You: _____

Director: _____

You: _____

Director: _____

WORD PLAY

Complete the sentences below with the *appropriate* word from the Word List. You can use some words in more than one sentence.

Sentences

a. Do you have a _____?

b. They play on the _____.

c. They play with the _____.

d. The child uses the _____.

e. She draws with a _____.

Word List

1. cookie	11. crayon
2. brush	12. puzzle
3. seesaw	13. pencil
4. pail	14. blanket
5. pencil sharpener	15. doll
6. monkey bars	16. glove
7. ball	17. swing
8. ruler	18. scissors
9. paint	19. clay
10. kite	20. bat

READING: What To Look for in a Day Care Center

There are many different things to look for when choosing a day care center. The building and playground equipment should be safe. The kitchen, cots, and all rooms should be clean. There should be enough food for all the children and the food should be nutritious*. All buses should be in good condition. The driver should be licensed to drive a bus. There should be a teacher supervising* the children on each bus. All of the teachers should have state licenses.

You should meet the director before sending your child to the center. Many directors have different ideas about teaching. Some directors think that play is most important. Other directors think that reading and writing are most important. Ask the director about this and choose the day care center that is best for your child.

*nutritious — good for the health of the child
*supervising — watching

Just the Facts

Tell whether the following statements are true or false.

1. There are many different things to look for when choosing a day care center.
2. The playground equipment should be new.
3. The kitchen should be clean.
4. The food should be nutritious.
5. All buses should be green.
6. You should meet the director before sending your child to a day care center.
7. Choose the center that thinks play is important.

What Do You Think?

Answer the following questions.

1. Would you send your child to a day care center? Tell why or why not.
2. What is the most important thing to look for in a day care center?
3. What is most important to you: play, or reading and writing?
4. Do they have day care centers in your country? Describe them.

TALK IT OVER

Talk with other students in groups. Each group discusses which of the following day care centers they think is best. One person from each group reports to the class.

1. **Deer Park Center**

   Hot lunches, half-day classes, exciting play activities, free transportation.

2. **Metropolitan Day Care Center**

   State licensed teachers, small classes, air-conditioned, open all year, cookies and juice, full day only.

3. **Sunshine Day Care Center**

   Hot lunches, half-day and full-day, state licensed teachers, free transportation, early reading program.

4. **Friendship Child Development Center**

   New building, modern equipment, state licensed teachers, all hours.

DO IT

Look in the *Yellow Pages* of the telephone book for three different day care centers. Look under "Day Care Centers," "Nursery Schools," or "Kindergartens." Read the ads and list two things about each center below. Also write the name, address, and phone number for each center.

Day Care Center 1

Name

Address   Phone

1. _____

2. _____

Day Care Center 2

Name

Address   Phone

1. _____

2. _____

Day Care Center 3

Name

Address   Phone

1. _____

2. _____

FOR YOUR INFORMATION

A. There are many different kinds of day care centers:

1. Half-day centers

2. Full-day centers

3. Church-sponsored centers

4. Centers for handicapped children

Day care centers are usually sponsored by state or city governments. Usually you must pay the day care center. The amount you pay depends on the amount of money you earn.

For more information, call the Office of Child Development or the Mayor's Office of your city government. You can also look in the *Yellow Pages* of your telephone book under "Day Care Centers." You can also write to the Department of Health and Human Services, U.S. Government, Washington, D.C.

B. Nursery Schools:

These schools are private schools. They can be half-day or full-day. Nursery schools usually take children from two years old to five years old. Day care centers usually take children from one month to five years old. Nursery schools usually cost more than day care centers. These schools are listed in the *Yellow Pages* of your telephone book.

C. Family Day Care:

Family day care is different from day care centers. In family day care, children stay in private homes in small groups. Usually there are six children in a group.

REPAIRS:
APPLIANCES AND AUTO

Repairs: Appliances and Auto

A. Appliances
1. clerk
2. counter
3. television/T.V.
4. vacuum cleaner
5. carpet sweeper
6. radio
7. blender
8. air conditioner
9. sewing machine
10. electric coffee pot
11. cord
12. handle
13. plug
14. socket

B. Auto

1. mechanic
2. wrench
3. lift
4. muffler
5. tail pipe
6. car/auto/automobile
7. gas pump
8. air hose
9. tire gauge
10. tire
11. wheel/tire rim
12. trunk
13. bumper
14. fender
15. window
16. windshield
17. windshield wiper
18. hood
19. headlight
20. turn signal
21. door
22. handle
23. gas tank
24. oil

PRACTICE WITH PICTURES

Appliances

1.

razor/shaver

2.

mixer

3.

calculator

4.

toaster

5.

broiler/toaster oven

6.

can opener

7.

iron

8.

hair dryer/hair blower

9.
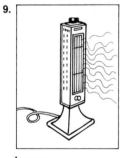
heater

10.
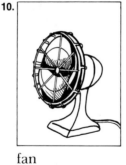
fan

11.

juicer

12.
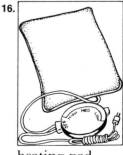
microwave oven

13.
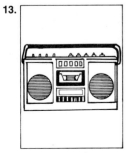
tape recorder

14.

vaporizer

15.
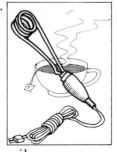
coil

16.
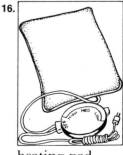
heating pad

PRACTICE WITH PICTURES

Auto

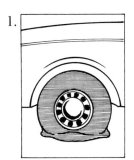

1.

flat tire

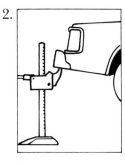

2.

jack

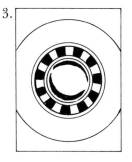

3.

hub cap

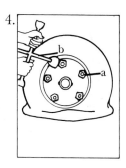

4.

a. lug
b. lug wrench

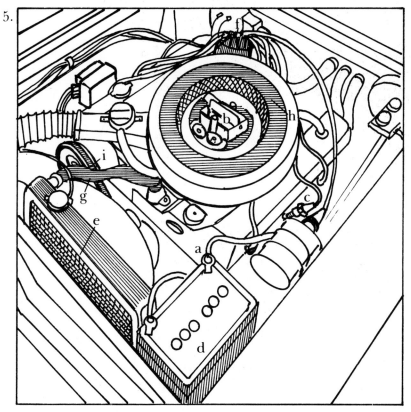

5.

a. engine
b. carburetor
c. spark plug
d. battery
e. radiator
f. distributor
g. hose
h. air filter
i. fan belt

Under the Hood

CONVERSATION 1: The Broken Vacuum Cleaner

1.

A. My vacuum cleaner is broken.
B. How long have you had it?
A. I've had it since January.

2.

B. Good, it's still under warranty. That means it won't cost you anything.

3.

B. What's the problem?
A. It won't start.

4.

A. What's wrong with it?
B. It could be the motor or the switch.

5.

A. Do I have to leave it?
B. No, I'll check it now.

6.

B. You need a new switch.
A. How long will it take?
B. Half an hour. You can wait here.

CONVERSATION 2: The Broken Muffler

1.

A. Do you hear a noise?
B. Yes, it sounds bad. Let's
   stop at the next gas station.

2.

A. Is there a mechanic on duty?
C. Yes, he's inside.

3.

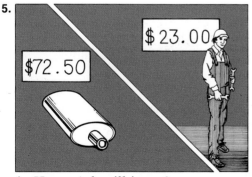

A. When I drive I hear a loud
   noise.
D. Let's take a look.

4.

D. The muffler is broken.
A. Can you fix it?
D. No, you need a new one.

5.

A. How much will it cost?
D. $72.50 for the muffler and
   $23.00 for labor.

6.

A. When will it be ready?
D. Tomorrow at one o'clock.
A. Fine, I'll be back tomorrow.

CONVERSATION PLUS

Use the words in parentheses in each sentence below to make new sentences.

1. My **vacuum cleaner** is broken. (*toaster, can opener, television, radio*)
2. I've had it since **January**. (*February, March, April, May, June, July, August, September, October, November, December*)
3. It won't **start**. (*go, move, work*)
4. It could be the **motor** or the **switch**. (*carburetor . . . spark plugs, radiator . . . hose, battery . . . cable*)
5. I'll check it **now**. (*right away, soon, at one o'clock, tomorrow*)
6. It sounds **bad**. (*terrible, awful, horrible*)
7. You need a new **one**. (*muffler, battery, engine, fan belt, hose*)
8. Yes, he's **inside**. (*outside, over here, over there, in the office*)

WHAT'S RIGHT?

Make the *appropriate* choice. Choose a, b, or c for each number below.

1. How long have you had it?
   - ☐ a. Tomorrow at one o'clock.
   - ☐ b. You can wait here.
   - ☐ c. Since January.

2. What's the problem?

☐ a. It won't cost you
    anything.

☐ b. It won't start.

☐ c. Yes, it sounds bad.

3. Do I have to leave it?

☐ a. No, I'll check it now.

☐ b. It won't cost you
    anything.

☐ c. It won't start.

4. ☐ a. What's the problem?

   ☐ b. How long will it take?

   ☐ c. How much will it cost?

Half an hour.

5. ☐ a. Do you hear a noise?

   ☐ b. What's the problem?

   ☐ c. Can you fix it?

No, you need a new one.

6. ☐ a. Is there a mechanic on duty?

   ☐ b. How much will it cost?

   ☐ c. Do I have to leave it?

$72.50 for the muffler and
$23.00 for labor.

YOUR TURN

Fill in each blank with an *appropriate* question or answer.

1. A. How long have you had it?
   B. _____

2. A. _____
   B. It won't start.

3. A. Do I have to leave it?
   B. _____

4. A. Do you hear a noise?
   B. _____

5. A. Is there a mechanic on duty?
   B. _____

6. A. _____
   B. No, you need a new one.

7. A. _____
   B. $72.50 for the muffler and $23.00 for labor.

8. A. When will it be ready?
   B. _____

ROLE PLAY

1. Your television is broken. It's still under warranty. You take it to the appliance repair store and tell the problem to the clerk. The clerk tells you what is wrong with it and when he can fix it.

You: _____

Clerk: _____

You: _____

Clerk: _____

You: _____

Clerk: _____

2. You have a problem with your car battery. You take it to the garage and ask the mechanic what to do. He tells you what you need and how much it will cost.

You: _____

Mechanic: _____

You: _____

Mechanic: _____

You: _____

Mechanic: _____

WORD PLAY

Choose the word that is *inappropriate* in each group.

1. vacuum cleaner, hair dryer, headlight, iron
2. cord, handle, plug, mixer
3. trunk, hood, door, wrench
4. wrench, mechanic, jack, tire gauge
5. broiler, electric coffee pot, toaster, carpet sweeper
6. carburetor, battery, door, radiator
7. carpet sweeper, spark plug, fan belt, engine
8. mixer, toaster, blender, distributor

READING: The Warranty

A warranty is a promise in writing from a company to fix or replace any item that is not working properly. The warranty is for a certain period of time. This time is usually for one, two, or three years. An auto warranty is usually for one or two years or a certain number of miles. *For example*: The Continental Car Company promises to fix the transmission and engine if either one is defective* for one year or 12,000 miles. (Whichever comes first.)

A guarantee is the same as a warranty. When you purchase a car or a new appliance, ask about the warranty or guarantee. Ask how long the warranty is for and what parts are guaranteed. A warranty card comes with the item. Fill out the information on the card and send it to the company. This tells the company when and where you bought the item. The company is only responsible for defective parts. It is not responsible if the buyer drops the item or does not use it properly. A warranty protects the buyer and the company.

*defective — badly made

Catching On

Answer the following questions.

1. What is a warranty?
2. How long is a warranty usually for?
3. Give an example of an auto warranty.
4. What is a guarantee?
5. What information should you ask about the warranty?
6. What should you do with a warranty card?
7. What does the information on the warranty card tell the company?
8. Is the company responsible for an item if you don't use that item properly?

What Do You Think?

Answer the following questions.

1. Should a company give warranties? Tell why or why not.
2. How long should a warranty last? Why?
3. Should a company be responsible if you drop the item?
4. Are there warranties in your country?

TALK IT OVER

Talk with other students in groups. Read the descriptions of the four television sets below. Each group discusses which set they think is best. One person from each group reports to the class.

Television 1

This set has a 9-inch screen. It has excellent color. It doesn't have an automatic channel selector. It weighs 20 pounds. It costs $345.00. It has a one-year warranty.

Television 2

This set has a 12-inch screen. It has an automatic channel selector. The color is fair. It weighs 28 pounds. It costs $400.00. It has a two-year warranty.

Television 3

This set has a 7-inch screen. It has good color. It doesn't have an automatic channel selector. It weighs 13 pounds. It costs $300.00. It has a two-year warranty.

Television 4

This set has a 19-inch screen. It has excellent color. There is an automatic channel selector. It weighs 54 pounds. It costs $600.00. It has a three-year warranty.

DO IT

Look at the sample letter below. Study the different parts of the letter. Write a letter like this. Tell about an appliance you bought. Tell where and when you bought it. Tell what's wrong with it and ask what to do.

1624 Fremont Street
Ames, Iowa 60257 ← **Return Address**

Nov. 21, 1984 ← **Date**

NBA Radio Company
19 Benson Street
Portland, Oregon 96789 ← **Address**

Dear Sir: ← **Salutation**

  I bought a clock radio at the Fox Department Store on August 15, 1984. The clock doesn't work but the radio does. The item is under warranty. ← **Body**

  Please tell me where I can get it fixed.

Sincerely Yours, ←**Closing**

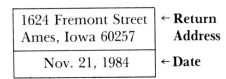

Chris Curtis ← **Signature**

FOR YOUR INFORMATION

A. Warranties:

    1. Make a list of all your appliances. On this list, write the name of the store, the date you bought the appliance, the serial number* on the appliance and the number on the warranty card. Keep the list to help you when you have a complaint.

    2. Always ask for an estimate in writing before you let anyone fix your appliance or auto.

    3. Send in the warranty card for any item immediately.

B. Complaints:

    1. If you have a complaint and the company or store does not help you, call the Better Business Bureau. This telephone number is listed in the *White Pages* of your telephone book.

    2. If you have a complaint you can also call the Office of Consumer Affairs. This number is listed in the *White Pages* of your telephone book.

    3. If your car is still under warranty and doesn't work, go to the place where you bought it. If they won't help you, call or write the factory. Ask for the Customer Service Department. This address is listed in the Instruction Book that comes with the auto.

*serial number — an identification number printed on the bottom or side of an appliance

Appendix

1. <u>Letters</u>

A, a, B, b, C, c, D, d, E, e, F, f, G, g, H, h, I, i,
J, j, K, k, L, l, M, m, N, n, O, o, P, p, Q, q, R, r,
S, s, T, t, U, u, V, v, W, w, X, x, Y, y, Z, z

2. <u>Numbers</u>

1	one	30	thirty
2	two	31	thirty-one
3	three	40	forty
4	four	41	forty-one
5	five	50	fifty
6	six	51	fifty-one
7	seven	60	sixty
8	eight	61	sixty-one
9	nine	70	seventy
10	ten	71	seventy-one
11	eleven	80	eighty
12	twelve	81	eighty-one
13	thirteen	90	ninety
14	fourteen	91	ninety-one
15	fifteen	100	one hundred
16	sixteen	101	one hundred one (one oh one)
17	seventeen	1,000	one thousand
18	eighteen	1,001	one thousand one
19	nineteen	1,010	one thousand ten
20	twenty	100,000	one hundred thousand
21	twenty-one	1,000,000	one million

3. <u>Colors</u>

red, orange, yellow, green, blue, pink, white, black, gray, purple

4. Days of the Week

Sunday, Monday, Tuesday, Wednesday, Thursday, Friday, Saturday
Sun.   Mon.   Tues.   Wed.   Thur.   Fri.   Sat.

5. Months

January, February, March, April, May, June, July, August, September, October.
Jan.   Feb.   Mar.   Apr.   May   Jun.   Jul.   Aug.   Sept.   Oct.
November, December
Nov.   Dec.

6. Seasons

summer, fall/autumn, winter, spring
summer—June, July, August
fall—September, October, November
winter—December, January, February
spring—March, April, May

7. Holidays

Those holidays marked with an asterisk are federal legal holidays and are observed in most states of the U.S.

*New Year's Day, January 1: the first day of the new calendar year
  Lincoln's Birthday, February 12: celebrating the birthday of President
      Abraham Lincoln
  Valentine's Day, February 14: celebrating Saint Valentine and love
*Washington's Birthday, February 22: celebrating the birthday of President
      George Washington
  Saint Patrick's Day, March 17: celebrating the patron saint of Ireland. It's the
      American custom to honor the Irish and wear green on this day.
  Mothers' Day, date varies in May: honoring mothers
*Memorial Day, the last Monday in May: honoring all people who have died in
      the service of the armed forces of the United States
  Fathers' Day, date varies in June: honoring fathers
*July Fourth/Independence Day: commemorating United States independence
      from England
*Labor Day, the first Monday in September: honoring all laborers in the United
      States
*Columbus Day, October 12: honoring the birthday of Christopher Columbus,
      credited with discovering America

Halloween, October 31: the Eve of All Saints' Day; a holiday celebrated mostly by children, who dress up as witches and ghosts.

Election Day, the first Tuesday after the first Monday in November: all citizens of the United States have the opportunity to vote on this day.

*Veterans' Day, November 11: honoring all people who have served in the armed forces of the United States.

*Thanksgiving Day, the 4th Thursday in November: commemorating the Pilgrims' first harvest in the New World and their thanksgiving to God for protecting their settlement in Plymouth, Massachusetts.

*Christmas Day, December 25: celebration of the birth of Christ. People exchange gifts on this day.

8. The Names of the States and Capitals

Alabama (Montgomery)
Alaska (Juneau)
Arizona (Phoenix)
Arkansas (Little Rock)
California (Sacramento)
Colorado (Denver)
Connecticut (Hartford)
Delaware (Dover)
Florida (Tallahassee)
Georgia (Atlanta)
Hawaii (Honolulu)
Idaho (Boise)
Illinois (Springfield)
Indiana (Indianapolis)
Iowa (Des Moines)
Kansas (Topeka)
Kentucky (Frankfort)

Louisiana (Baton Rouge)
Maine (Augusta)
Maryland (Annapolis)
Massachusetts (Boston)
Michigan (Lansing)
Minnesota (St. Paul)
Mississippi (Jackson)
Missouri (Jefferson City)
Montana (Helena)
Nebraska (Lincoln)
Nevada (Carson City)
New Hampshire (Concord)
New Jersey (Trenton)
New Mexico (Santa Fe)
New York (Albany)
North Carolina (Raleigh)
North Dakota (Bismarck)

Ohio (Columbus)
Oklahoma (Oklahoma City)
Oregon (Salem)
Pennsylvania (Harrisburg)
Rhode Island (Providence)
South Carolina (Columbia)
South Dakota (Pierre)
Tennessee (Nashville)
Texas (Austin)
Utah (Salt Lake City)
Vermont (Montpelier)
Virginia (Richmond)
Washington (Olympia)
West Virginia (Charleston)
Wisconsin (Madison)
Wyoming (Cheyenne)

9. Names of the Presidents

George Washington
John Adams
Thomas Jefferson
James Madison
James Monroe
John Quincy Adams

Andrew Jackson
Martin Van Buren
William Henry Harrison
John Tyler
James K. Polk
Zachary Taylor

Millard Fillmore
Franklin Pierce
James Buchanan
Abraham Lincoln
Andrew Johnson
Ulysses S. Grant

Rutherford B. Hayes

James A. Garfield

Chester A. Arthur

Grover Cleveland

Benjamin Harrison

Grover Cleveland (second term)

William McKinley

Theodore Roosevelt

William Howard Taft

Woodrow Wilson

Warren G. Harding

Calvin Coolidge

Herbert C. Hoover

Franklin D. Roosevelt

Harry S. Truman

Dwight D. Eisenhower

John F. Kennedy

Lyndon B. Johnson

Richard M. Nixon

Gerald R. Ford

Jimmy Carter

Ronald Reagan